WASTE FREE KITCHEN HANDBOOK

A guide to eating well and saving
money by wasting less food

DANA GUNDERS

CHRONICLE BOOKS

SAN FRANCISCO

For my dad, who can suck meat off a chicken bone like no one else.
For my mom, who has been reusing tea bags for as long as I can remember.
For my sister Debi, who reigns as the queen of kitchen concoctions.
For my husband Jose, who completes me, and my plate.
For the growing army of passionate food-waste warriors who love food as much as I do.

Library of Congress Cataloging-in-Publication
Data available.

ISBN 978-1-4521-3354-6

Manufactured in China

MIX
Paper from
responsible sources
FSC™ C008047

Designed by Walter C. Baumann

10 9 8 7 6 5 4 3 2

Chronicle Books LLC
680 Second Street
San Francisco, California 94107
www.chroniclebooks.com

Contents

Acknowledgments

It takes a village to shepherd a book from concept to bookstore. I'm enormously grateful to the people of that village, only some of whom I'm able to mention here.

First, to the Natural Resources Defense Council for helping in so many ways to make this book a reality. Special thanks to Jonathan Kaplan for his guidance and encouragement; Peter Lehner and Doug Barasch for their early support for the project; Michele Egan for her design eye; Irina Petrova for her endurance; Jenny Powers, Jackie Wei, Lisa Goffredi, Lisa Benenson, and Alex Kennaugh for their strategic advice and outreach; Erik Olson for helping make it a success; and the many staff for bravely testing recipes!

Next, to all the hands that helped research and write this book: Kristina Johnson for her creative take on recipes, Keri Keifer for her extensive research, Andrea Spacht for always pitching in, Jason Fitzroy Jeffers for getting the ball rolling on food scraps, Kate Slate for her delightful nature and wise recipe advice, Helen Rogan for keen editing, and Mike Ryan for his veterinary advice. Special thanks to Don Schaffner at Rutgers University for ensuring all the recommendations in the book are safe ones.

Sarah Malarkey, Lorena Jones, Sarah Billingsley, Dawn Yanagihara, Peter Perez, David Hawk, and my agent Kari Stuart—thank you for all your work to make this book a reality. Susan Grode, your staunch support was invaluable.

Finally, huge appreciation for Anita and Josh Bekenstein, Jesse and Betsy Fink, and Eliza Brown and family for believing in NRDC's ability to make a dent in food waste and actively supporting our work.

MAKING A DIFFERENCE

Food-waste warriors don't plot and fight. We pickle and freeze.

My journey to becoming a food-waste warrior started at work, where I was researching how to improve farming. My aim was to help farmers use less water, fertilizers, and pesticides. But what I found startled me. After all the effort and resources that were being invested to get food to our plates, a huge amount of it was going uneaten! It occurred to me that no matter how organically or sustainably we grow our food, if it doesn't get eaten, it doesn't do anyone any good.

About 40 percent of all food in the United States does not get eaten.[1] That's crazy! It's like buying five bags of groceries and then dropping two of the bags in the grocery store parking lot and not bothering to pick them up.

Collectively, consumers are responsible for more wasted food than farmers, grocery stores, or any other part of the food supply chain. The lettuce that went bad, the leftovers you never got around to eating, and that scary science experiment in the back of the refrigerator you're hoping will disappear—it all adds up. Think about it. If you don't eat half of that fish you paid $10 for, that's $5 you're throwing away. In fact, Americans are throwing away an average of $120 each month per household of four in the form of uneaten food.[2] That's real money going straight into the garbage instead of paying off your credit card bills or adding to your savings account.

It hasn't always been this way. Today, we waste 50 percent more food in the United States than we did even in the 1970s.[3] We also waste 10 times more than the average consumer in Southeast Asia.[4] A woman from Hong Kong once told me that when she was a child, her aunts and uncles would inspect her bowl and tell her that each morsel of rice she had left would turn into a mole on the face of her future husband! Can you imagine if we thought that way about food in our own lives?

The good news is that turning around the food-waste trend is not only doable, it can actually improve your experience with food. Wasting less food is about keeping ingredients fresh. It's about sleek menus that use up different parts of animals and vegetables. It's about getting creative with what you have, and getting to know your food—how it ages and how it is best stored. All this only adds to the enjoyment of eating.

This book arms you with the tools you need so that you can too become a food-waste warrior. It's chock-full of useful information about getting the most out of the food you buy, better ways to store food, the secret truth behind so-called "expiration" dates on groceries, tricks to tell when food has actually gone bad, and how to start composting.

Food is simply too good to waste. Together we can make a major dent in what's currently getting tossed—and put a little cash back in our wallets at the same time.

Where Food Is Wasted, from Farm to French Fries

Food can be lost at each point on its journey to you. On the farm, crops are sometimes left unharvested because they're not the right size or shape to meet grocery store standards. On the boat, fish are thrown overboard because fishermen exceed their catch quota or they catch unwanted species. Distribution centers have leftover inventory. Grocery stores carry a multitude of products, some of which inevitably spoil.

In restaurants, large portions, large menus, and poor training for food handlers contribute to food waste. In 1955, McDonald's introduced a new product line: French fries. The original portion weighed 2.4 oz/68 g and had 210 calories. Today, that product is the small size and is normally overlooked for the large weighing in at 5.9 oz/ 167 g and 610 calories.[5] What's more, the largest order of french fries in the United States is 11 percent larger than the largest size available in the United Kingdom.[6]

McDonald's is not alone. Portion sizes are now sometimes 2 to 8 times larger than the standard serving sizes defined by the U.S. Department of Agriculture and the Food and Drug Administration.[7] From 1982 to 2002, the number of calories in the average slice of pizza grew by 70 percent, doubled for the average chicken Caesar salad, and *quadrupled* for the average chocolate chip cookie.[8] The chart that follows lists the increase in calories for other popular foods between 1982 and 2002.

Growing Portion Sizes, 1982 to 2002

	PORTION SIZE IN 1982		PORTION SIZE IN 2002		PERCENTAGE GROWTH
	PORTION	CALORIES	PORTION	CALORIES	
Pepperoni pizza	1 large slice	500	1 large slice	850	70%
Cheeseburger	1	333	1	590	77%
Chicken Caesar salad	1½ cups/150 g	390	3½ cups/350 g	790	103%
Spaghetti with meatballs	1 cup/50 g with sauce, 3 small meatballs	500	2 cups/100 g with sauce, 3 large meatballs	1,020	104%
Large popcorn	5 cups/40 g	270	11 cups/90 g	630	133%
Blueberry muffin	1½ oz/40 g	210	5 oz/140 g	500	138%
Bagel	3-in/8-cm diameter	140	6-in/15-cm diameter	350	150%
Soda	6½ oz/190 ml	82	20 oz/590 ml	250	205%
Chocolate chip cookie	1½-in/4-cm diameter	55	3½-in/9-cm diameter	275	400%

Source: National Heart, Lung, and Blood Institute, "Portion Distortion 1" (2003) and "Portion Distortion 2" (2004), www.nhlbi.nih.gov/health/public/heart/obesity/wecan/eat-right/portion-distortion.htm.

What Contributes to Food Waste in Homes

Consumers—you and I—throw food out for all sorts of reasons.

Does this sound familiar? On your weekend grocery trip, you bought spinach in the hopes you would kick-start your new health regime. But then spinach just didn't look satisfying on Monday night. You also bought some chicken to try a new recipe that you read in a magazine. But you didn't have time on Tuesday to actually do all the prep work *and* you realized you had forgotten to buy a key ingredient. On Wednesday, colleagues were going out for drinks after work and you decided that jalapeño poppers would cover for dinner that night. Thursday you were too tired to cook and ordered pizza. By Friday, the spinach had started to turn yellow and the chicken looked a little suspect. So you tossed them both before the trash was picked up.

Generally speaking, the reasons we waste food in our homes fall into a few categories.

Wishful thinking: Having busy weeks like the one just described is par for the course for many of us. And while we might not want to admit that we aren't living the dream of growing organic herbs in the window and cooking healthful meals from scratch each night, we should. If we were more realistic at the grocery store about the constraints on our time, we would probably be more modest in our food purchases. Later, I'll offer some great tips for how to plan meals, make better shopping lists, cook when you have the time, freeze food for future uses, and other food-saving ideas.

Too-large portion sizes: The portion size explosion is not only in restaurants, but also in homes. The surface area of the average dinner plate expanded by 36 percent between 1960 and 2007.[9] Even our trusty cookbooks are bending to our growing stomachs. The iconic cookbook *Joy of Cooking* has increased its portion sizes by 33.2 percent since 1996. In other words, a recipe that used to serve 12 people now serves 9 people (or the ingredient amounts are greater for the same number of servings).[10] Let's face it. There are only two things that are happening with these extra calories. Either we're

Food Recovery Hierarchy

MOST PREFERRED

Create Less Surplus

Feed People in Need

Feed Animals

Industrial Uses

Compost

Incineration or Landfill

LEAST PREFERRED

Source: Adapted from U.S. Environmental Protection Agency.

eating them or we're throwing them out, presenting a choice between your waist and your waste. I'll offer some shortcuts to help you cook the right amounts, so you don't wind up with unnecessarily huge portions or more leftovers than you'd like.

Lack of kitchen know-how: Your great-grandma probably knew how to can tomatoes. Do you? She also knew how to tell when the yogurt was bad without looking at the date, because back then there were no dates. She probably bought whole chickens and used up all the parts, even making her own chicken stock with the bones.

Along with our attitudes about food, our knowledge of food has changed over the years. Home economics is no longer offered in many schools, and the number of meals eaten outside the home almost doubled between 1978 and 2008.[11] We don't have to go back to making everything from scratch, but we do need to re-learn some basic food skills that will reduce food waste. Here you'll learn ways to store food and keep food fresher longer, and easy recipes for using all the bits and pieces of food in the fridge.

Food Recovery Hierarchy for Home Kitchens

MOST PREFERRED

Shop with a list and with restraint

Store food well; cook planned meals

Practice emergency use-it-up measures; freeze

The dog scores

Compost/in-sink disposal

Garbage

LEAST PREFERRED

All waste is not equal: Some foods represent much more in the way of resources than others, and meat products tend to be among the heaviest resource users. In fact, producing animal products requires 4 to 40 times more calories than they provide in nutrition.[12] So chucking out a cut of top sirloin has a different impact than tossing out a bunch of carrots. The best place to start wasting less is with meat products. After that, dairy packs the most punch in terms of resources saved. I'll lay out more about what is most wasteful and help you get started with composting.

The U.S. Environmental Protection Agency created a Food Recovery Hierarchy for municipalities and businesses (above left) to guide their thinking about waste. It essentially applies the "reduce, reuse, recycle" mantra to food waste.

The same principles can help us establish a waste-less mindset for our homes. I've translated the idea into something a little more useful for home kitchens (above right). As you go about your week and through your refrigerator, keep this hierarchy in mind to help guide you.

What It Takes to Produce Food

Does it even matter if we waste food?

Yes. Wasting food has staggering ecological implications when you consider all the resources that go into growing it.

About half the land area in the United States is used for agriculture.[13] Around the world, agriculture has also driven conversion of rain forest and native grasslands into croplands at an alarming rate. If we could meet some of our food needs by capturing food that is currently wasted, we might ultimately help prevent even more natural land from being plowed under.

Agriculture also uses 70 percent of the fresh water in the United States.[14] In fact, it takes the same amount of water to produce a hamburger as it does to take a 90-minute shower![15] The chart on the facing page shows how many minutes you would have to shower to use the amount of water required to produce each of the products listed. It takes into account all of the water needed to irrigate crops (including feed crops for livestock), the water needed to clean out facilities where products are processed, and any other water that might be used in getting the products to your table.

In addition to the land and water it uses, agriculture releases hundreds of millions of pounds of pesticides and fertilizers into our environment, is the leading cause of poor water quality in our nation's rivers and streams, and is a large emitter of two potent greenhouse gases responsible for warming our climate: nitrous oxide and methane. In fact, it's estimated that in the United States, greenhouse gas emissions from uneaten food are equivalent to that of 33 million passenger vehicles. When food doesn't get eaten, this is all for naught.

Water Required to Produce Certain Products, in Shower Minutes

PRODUCT	QUANTITY	WATER USE EQUIVALENT IN SHOWER MINUTES 🌢 = 10 SHOWER MINUTES	
Beer	8 oz/240 ml	4	
Tomato	1 lb/455 g	5	
Wine	4 oz/120 ml	6	
Milk	8 oz/240 ml	6	
Potato	1 lb/455 g	7	
Egg	1 egg	11	
Banana	1 lb/455 g	42	
Apple	1 lb/455 g	43	
Pasta, dry	1 lb/455 g	44	
Rice, white	1 lb/455 g	60	
Personal pizza	26 oz/735 g	67	
Chocolate	4 oz/115 g	90	
Chicken	1 lb/455 g	104	
Cheese	1 lb/455 g	122	
Pork	1 lb/455 g	144	
Beef	1 lb/455 g	370	

Source: Water Footprint Network, Product Gallery Water Footprint Estimates, www.waterfootprint.org. Note: These estimates are for total water use, including naturally occurring rain, otherwise known as "green water." The Water Footprint Network includes this water because it would otherwise have fed aquifers or reservoirs or been part of other natural processes, and instead is not available for those uses. In addition, note that these estimates reflect a global average, but water use varies by geography and production methods. They assume a shower that uses 5 gl/19 L per 1 minute, which is twice that of a new showerhead purchased today and triple that of a low-flow showerhead.

In the end, the vast majority of food waste ends up in landfills or incinerators. In the United States, less than 5 percent of discarded food is composted.[16] Food now represents the single largest component of municipal solid waste brought to landfills, where it also releases methane, a greenhouse gas 34 times more potent than carbon dioxide. And if that weren't enough, it costs Americans $1.5 billion a year just to dispose of the wasted food.[17]

The impacts of food waste are not limited to the United States, however. The footprint of food that is lost or wasted across the globe is estimated as follows.

- **28 percent** of all agricultural land—an area larger than Canada[18]

- **38 times the volume** of water used by all U.S. households[19]

- **3.3 billion metric tons** of carbon dioxide equivalent; if it were a country, uneaten food would be *third* in its greenhouse gas footprint, after the United States and China[20]

All that for food that never gets eaten!

Wasting Less Food Saves Resources and Money—and Might Even Save Lives

World hunger is another reason to care about food waste. There are 842 million people in the world suffering from chronic hunger.[21] We produce enough food today to feed them all—4,600 calories per person per day worldwide—but ultimately only 2,000 calories to 2,800 calories per person are available for consumption.[22] And even that is not getting to those who need it most.

With more than 9 billion people expected on the planet in 2050, and diets that are increasingly dependent on meat, the challenge of feeding ourselves will only become more difficult. The United Nations forecasts that we'll need up to 60 percent more food to feed that projected population.[23] To achieve this, it estimates that about another 170 million acres of farmland will be required, along with a significant increase in yields from existing croplands in developing countries, putting even more strain on already limited natural resources such as fresh water.[24] All of these estimates assume no reduction in the amount of food that is wasted.

There is a huge opportunity to meet some of our global food needs by reducing the amount of food that goes uneaten. Some experts believe that cutting food losses in half could cover 22 percent of the gap in future food needs.[25] Reducing the amount of food that is wasted will also reduce pressure to intensify production on existing cropland or convert natural land to food production. One projection estimates that reducing food waste at the consumer level by 30 percent could save roughly 100 million acres of cropland by 2030.[26]

Much of the world has already caught on to the importance of food conservation. In January 2012, the European Parliament adopted a resolution to reduce food waste by 50 percent by 2020 and designated 2014 as the European Year Against Food Waste. Its members said, "The most important problem in the future will be to tackle increased demand for food, as it will outstrip supply. We can no longer afford to stand by while perfectly edible food is wasted. This is an ethical but also an economic and social problem, with huge implications for the environment."[27]

In the United States, reducing losses by one-third would save enough food to equal the total diets of all 50 million food-insecure Americans—if only this food could actually be captured and distributed to them.[28]

No One's Perfect—Just Get Started on the Journey

One day while writing this book, after many hours in a coffee shop, I ordered a sandwich. It came with a salad drenched in dressing, and I mean *drenched*. I couldn't eat it. I stared down, laughing at the irony. There I was, with a plate of food in front of me that would give me the energy to continue writing about not wasting food, and I couldn't avoid wasting that food.

That incident reminded me to remind my readers that this book is really about a journey. It's not going to stop all your waste tomorrow, even if you read every page and practice every tip. Food will still go to waste, but you *can* make a dent.

Wasting less is not rocket science. It doesn't require any gadgets either. While the collective impacts of wasting less food are big, the action is about small, easy changes you can make in your daily food rhythm that will streamline your consumption.

Making those changes is the journey. It won't be perfect. Milk will go sour, and dressing-drenched salad will get left on plates. Don't be too hard on yourself! And enjoy trying new tricks and recipes along the way. Make it a game to see just how little you can throw in the trash. The more you enjoy the steps suggested in this book, the more likely you are to incorporate them into your regular kitchen act.

Let's get to it!

PART ONE

STRATEGIES FOR EVERYDAY LIFE

Our habits around getting food on our plates are core to how much food we use—and how much we don't. The secret to wasting less food is integrating small, easy steps into your current routine. In this section, you'll find information on such steps, including shopping, storing, cooking, evaluating, and even disposal. Take from these pages those ideas that are most helpful to you in creating a recipe for wasting less food in your daily life.

Sage Shopping

The supermarket is ground zero for food waste. It's where the real commitment to food is made, whether you end up eating it or not.

You might think you threw away that bag of salad greens because it went bad. But why did it go bad? Most likely, you didn't do a good job of matching your shopping trip to the reality of your week. So as with other commitments in your life, when you're buying (and thus committing to) food, choose wisely.

Tricks of the Grocery Trade

The basic advice is easy to grasp and much, much harder to practice: Plan your meals, make a shopping list from that plan, and stick to the list—and then stick to the plan.

If you can honestly say you do all of that, by all means just skim this chapter. Let's face it, though. Many of us walk out of the store with way more than we need, and more than we wind up actually getting through during the week. In fact, during the average shopping trip, 55 percent of purchases—more than half—are unplanned.[29]

I know these unplanned purchases firsthand. I run to the store for eggs and leave with a fresh baguette (it smelled so good), some fancy cheese (it was on sale and goes with the baguette), frozen yogurt (there was a new flavor to try), and a few cans of diced tomatoes (while I was there).

Don't despair! One of the key findings of this research is that those who have a plan and a shopping list are least likely to stray from their intended purchases.[30] Even if you're not someone who tends to plan out your meals for the week, you will still find quick planning ideas in this chapter that can help you organize your purchases.

You'll also find a bunch of tips that may help you trick yourself into buying less. If using a large shopping cart leads you to purchase more, how about shopping without a cart? If using credit cards encourages a higher average total at the checkout, why not pay with cash? The "Shopping Guidelines" section in this chapter lays out several of these tricks.

At the same time, we as consumers also influence store behavior. The grocery business is ferociously competitive. More than anything, stores want us to walk through their doors, and they are willing to go to great lengths to ensure our satisfaction. Enabling the customer to always be right and accommodating our every expectation is actually leading to quite a bit of waste as well.

For instance, in his book *American Wasteland*, Jonathan Bloom describes his conversation with a grocery store about its rotisserie chickens. They estimated that over the course of a day, about *half* of their chickens are thrown out! Many are from the last batch of the night, since they don't want to disappoint that late-evening customer who wants to buy a chicken right before closing time. However, if customers came to understand that the store might run out of rotisserie chickens at the end of the evening, waste from that last batch might be avoided.

In addition to helping us match our shopping to our eating, this chapter will also highlight opportunities for us to help stores, and even the farms that supply them, waste less in their own operations. It's in our interest to help, since the cost of food that goes to waste in the store is ultimately built into the prices we pay.

Meal Planning

Grocery shopping without a plan is a bit like going somewhere new without directions. If you're lucky, you might go straight to your destination, but it's much more likely that you'll take a few unintended side trips along the way.

I'm a terrible planner, and I'm not just talking about meals. Budgeting, scheduling social activities, and following work project plans are not my strengths. So the idea that I'm going to plan out what to eat for the week before I even go to the store, and then actually stick to that plan, is a challenge for me. Unfortunately, there's no getting around the fact that some level of planning helps reduce waste. If you skip the planning step, you're almost guaranteed to end up with shriveled vegetables at some point.

Besides saving on wasted food, meal planning saves time, stress, and money and typically means healthier eating. Industry research shows that the one quarter of Americans who use written shopping lists and execute according to plan also make fewer impulse buys, have the lowest grocery bills, and make the fewest number of weekly trips to the store.[31] Add to that the fact that planning meals encourages a more well-rounded, nutritious diet and it's clear that planning has benefits that go far beyond reducing waste.

Ten Key Elements of Meal Planning

While it may be obvious that meal planning involves choosing meals to eat for the week and creating a shopping list for those meals, a handful of not-so-obvious tips can make the process more effective.

1. **Don't start from scratch.** No one is scoring you on your creativity. Meal planning does not mean hours with cookbooks every week. You likely already have a few meals that are regulars in your household. Count those in. Repeat them every week or two. Then, if you're up for it, try something new once in a while.

2. **Check the refrigerator.** Your refrigerator is the starting gate for planning the next week's meals. What needs using up? What's a good meal to make with the other half of that broccoli, the last of the cottage cheese, and the leftover pasta from two days ago? Sounds like a baked pasta dish might do the trick, and you'll need to buy some pasta sauce and mozzarella to make that work. Add those to the shopping list (after you've checked to be sure you don't have them in the pantry) and voilà. Meal one. Check.

3. **Use portion planners.** Use a portion calculator to figure out how much pasta or chicken or vegetables to make for your group size. Portion calculators are particularly helpful when you're feeding a bigger group, but they might also add some insight as to why you always wind up with extra rice. There are many on the Web to choose from; the "How Much Should I Make" chart on page 71 has some basic portion suggestions to get you started.

4. **Have kitchen essentials on hand.** Having two to three grains, cooking fundamentals, some key spices, and "hero" sauces that come to the rescue can bring new life to old meals. A list of recommended essentials can be found on page 67.

5. **Choose building blocks.** Pick two types of protein, one or two grains, and a vegetable medley that you can make at the beginning of the week and then incorporate into different meals. For instance, a sauté of broccoli and peppers can be used as a side one night,

spooned on enchiladas another night, and then worked into a soup or meatloaf later in the week. Brown rice or mashed potatoes could be incorporated into each of those meals as well. With different spices and sauces, it won't feel as though you're eating the same thing every night.

6. **Think double duty.** If you're planning for Tuesday taco night, what else could you use tortillas for? Maybe some Asian salad wraps later in the week, or those enchiladas? How about the cilantro? Unfortunately, the ingredients we need don't always come in the portions we need them in. Incorporating those ingredients into multiple meals will help you avoid the end-of-the-week overload. After you choose one meal, consider which ingredients come in large quantities, and plan a second meal around those.

7. **Schedule in a lazy night.** Or two or three. So often we go to the store with hopes and dreams of preparing fresh meals all week, but the reality is we don't have the time or energy to cook every night. So planning on lazy nights that don't involve cooking is key—whether you order in or take an already prepared food from the freezer. With my current crazy schedule, I plan to make only three meals each week. The rest are a combination of what's in the freezer, Thai takeout, and dinner with friends. This also helps make sure food doesn't get lost in the freezer for too long, since I know there are nights I'll be scrounging in there for dinner.

8. **Go fresh first.** For optimal nutrition and freshness, use perishables like fresh seafood and meat earlier in the week and make staples (pasta, dairy, omelets) later in the week. Some greens, such as kale and chard, will maintain their freshness longer than others.

9. **Lean on frozen ingredients.** I always keep a bunch of frozen vegetables on hand. They fill in the gaps, allowing me to buy only a handful of fresh vegetables that I know I will use each week, and helping me avoid going shopping late in the week if I've run out. From a health perspective, frozen foods have nearly all of the nutrients, and sometimes even more, of fresh. (See "Buying Frozen Foods," page 36.)

10. **Cook batches and freeze.** Soups, stews, casseroles, lasagna—all can be made in large batches, frozen, and defrosted when you're in need of a quick dinner on one of those lazy nights. Having these around saves you from having to plan *every* meal for the week. See the tips on freezing on page 52, and be sure to freeze in the amounts you'd want to defrost.

Want to skip all this planning stuff? Shop more often. Really, meal planning plays a critical role because we are buying food for a whole week and have to anticipate needs for all those meals. Shopping on a more frequent basis means you don't have to stock up on things and can rather buy just what suits your mood that day. No planning necessary. This might not work for everyone, depending on your available time and proximity to a market. But if you can make it happen, your meals will be fresher, planning will be less essential, and you may find you've added a little more flavor to your life.

Sample Weekly Dinner Meal Plan

SUNDAY	**Prepare some building blocks:** Cook chicken breasts, make a pot of brown rice, sauté a vegetable medley, chop onions and garlic for the week. **Dinner:** Chili (make a big pot), salad, fresh bread, cheese and onion garnish.
MONDAY	Chicken breasts stuffed with vegetables and cheese (same garnish as the night before), rice on the side.
TUESDAY	Pasta with pasta sauce and vegetable medley.
WEDNESDAY (LAZY NIGHT)	Something from the freezer, takeout, or a leftover smorgasbord.
THURSDAY	Chicken enchiladas (using leftover chicken breasts, vegetable medley, and chili). Freeze any chili that's still left.
FRIDAY	Go out with friends.
SATURDAY	Leftover smorgasbord, fill in with frozen items if needed. Freeze anything left over from the week.

Meal Plan Template

STEP 1: Foods that need using up	STEP 3: Meal Plan

		Breakfasts	Lunches	Dinners
	Sunday			
	Monday			
	Tuesday			
	Wednesday			
	Thursday			
	Friday			
	Saturday			

STEP 2: Dishes to make with these ingredients (Put these in lunch or early-week dinner slots.)

ingredients are required?	What components do I already have?	Components to buy (include quantities)

Don't forget to think double duty! You might need to take another look at your meals.

Shopping Guidelines

At the beginning of this book, I summarized the main reasons most of us waste food. A mismatch between shopping and eating is one. We simply buy more than we actually use. Whether you eat it or not, once you've bought food, you've committed your money as well as all the resources it took to grow that food. This means how you shop is really the most important factor in how much food you will waste.

The good news is that more careful grocery shopping immediately saves you money. There are also habits you can adopt that will help food last longer once you've brought it home. Finally, there are changes you can make that will help your stores and the farms that supply them waste less as well.

Resisting Temptation

The best way to align what you buy to what you use is to stick to your list. Sure, you might have forgotten to list something, but it's probably not that new flavor of chips that's buy-one-get-one-free at the end of the aisle. Don't be a stalwart about it. If you want to try those chips, by all means do. But when you're at the checkout counter, do a quick scan of your list versus your cart. Do you really need all those items that weren't on your list?

If you want to opt out of the subtle nuances the store uses to encourage purchases, you might try skipping the cart (you'll buy less if you have to carry it) and paying in cash (it makes the amount you're spending more tangible).[32] Even wearing headphones has been suggested, since the music in grocery stores is meant to encourage you to stay a while.

As for deals, there are a few ways to buy your milk and get one free without having to drink milkshakes all week. First, ask for rain checks. If an item is on sale but you don't need it at the moment, some stores will let you either buy it now and pick it up later, or buy it later at that sale price. Second, often stores give you deals on single items even if the promotion is for multiples. For instance, if yogurt is 10 for $10, it may still be 1 for $1. Read the fine print on the sign. Finally, don't assume that items specially displayed at the ends of aisles are good deals. Often they're not.

Buying the Right Amount

In the United Kingdom, households report that just under half of their wasted food is discarded because it was "not used in time"[33]—that is, it was not used before spoiling. If you think about your own household, some of the food you throw out is likely due to buying more than you need. Maybe you simply had to buy a particular size or quantity—such as a bunch of fresh herbs or a head of lettuce—even if you just needed a little bit. Doing your best to buy the portions you'll actually be using can help reduce waste at home.

One of the best ways to do this is to buy food from bulk bins that allow you to choose your own quantities. Not all stores have them, but where they're available, they can be particularly handy for items such as spices when you need only a small amount to make a recipe. Bringing your own bags or containers for these bins will cut down on plastic waste as well.

At the deli or meat counter, you can often have the employees cut things into the right portions for you. This can save money as well. For instance, you could buy one big roast and have the butcher remove the bone for soup, run half of it through the grinder for hamburger, and cut the rest into a pot roast. One super-market butcher estimated that this approach could save a customer about 30 percent, compared with buying separate cuts.[34]

This strategy can work for other foods too. Remember, stores are trying to keep you, their valued customer, happy. Only want half of a chunk of cheese? Ask them to cut it. Half loaf of bread? It can't hurt to ask!

If you need only a small amount of vegetables for a stir-fry or mixed vegetable recipe, try shopping the salad bar. Sure, you'll pay more per ounce, but it will probably add up to less than if you bought all those different items whole. And then you won't have to worry about the remainders wilting in your refrigerator.

Finally, if you're not sure what the right amount is, use a portion planner. Plenty of smartphone apps offer them now, so you can consult it right in the store aisle if you're unsure of how much to buy.

Keeping It Fresh

Part of eating the freshest foods is how you shop for them. Common sense prevails here. Buy perishables and frozen foods last so they spend the least amount of time at room temperature. Shake the water from the produce-aisle mister off your vegetables, because it will make them rot more quickly (and adds to their weight). And for goodness sake, don't let groceries sit in the car, particularly on a hot day! Try to make grocery shopping your last errand, or else keep a cooler in your trunk for the perishable and frozen goods. Then be sure to put them away as soon as you get them home.

Shopping at your farmers' market can also lead to fresher products, as they may not have had to travel as far, and thus may have been harvested more recently.

Buying Frozen Foods

Buying frozen foods can not only help you, your supermarket, and the whole supply chain waste less, it can make it easier to land healthful foods on your plate on a lazy night. Less food goes to waste when frozen, since it's not as perishable on the journey from the farm to your refrigerator. But are frozen foods as good for you as fresh foods? The consensus is, pretty much. Research shows that frozen fruits and vegetables have relatively equivalent nutrient profiles compared to fresh produce.[35, 36] In fact, because they are often picked at their peak freshness and frozen within hours of harvesting, they may in some cases have more nutrients than raw produce that travels for days and degrades in refrigerators. Frozen meat and fish are also good choices. As Harvard professor and chef Barton Seaver explained, "The technology of freezing fish has evolved to the point where it's comparable to, if not better than,

→>> Buy Funny Fruit!

Did you know that a huge amount of fruits and vegetables are never even harvested, just because they're the wrong shape, size, or color? And then more are thrown out before they leave the farm for the same reason. They could be perfectly nutritious and tasty, but if a cucumber is bent or a carrot has an extra arm, it won't make it to your grocery store shelves. Sometimes these imperfections are quite minor. One peach farmer told me, "For 8 out of 10 of the peaches I can't sell, you wouldn't even be able to tell me what's wrong with them!" Or, as another farmer put it, "If we picked our friends the way we selectively picked and culled our produce, we'd be very lonely."

Grocery stores believe we want only perfect-looking produce. Let's prove them wrong! Tell your grocery store you'd like them to carry fruit and vegetables with character. And when they do, be sure to cast your vote for those funny fruits with your dollar.

---

fresh fish."[37] In fact, frozen fish is delicious, economical, nutritious, and often better for the environment. The additional time allowed by freezing also means the fish can be shipped by land instead of air and enables fisherman to waste less at sea.[38]

Reducing Waste up the Chain

Choices we make as consumers can cause waste at the store or even at the farm. The most notable is our tendency to buy only attractive fruits and vegetables. Not all vegetables grow perfectly round, perfectly straight, or perfectly sized on the plant. Yet that's what we see on our grocery shelves—consistently perfect-looking produce—and that's what we tend to buy when presented with the option. Willingness to buy cosmetically challenged fruits and vegetables—or "funny fruit," as I like to call it—can help lead to less waste of fruit and vegetable crops at the farm. Perhaps that means choosing a peach that has a little bruise, or the smaller apples of the bunch. Sometimes these products will even be offered at a discount—or you could ask for one.

Buying the last of something can be helpful too. Many stores believe they'll sell more by creating an illusion of abundance. Think about it. When was the last time you went to a deli counter and saw the bowl of potato salad almost empty, or only a few apples in the produce section? Piles of produce, full bowls at the deli counter, entire fillets of salmon—this is the way products are presented, and it leads to a great deal of waste in stores.

But how are you supposed to buy the last of something when they never let it get that low? It's admittedly a bit of a chicken-and-egg situation. However, the more consumers show a willingness to buy things even when stocks are low, and have patience when items run out, the more supermarkets will be able to modify their practices to reduce in-store food waste.

Waste Diagnostics

Most of us waste more food than we realize. The best way to figure out how much you waste and where to focus your waste-reducing efforts is to conduct your own personal food-waste audit. Perhaps you always wind up throwing out leftovers, or you don't ever finish the vegetables you bought at the farmers' market.

Conducting a food-waste audit turns out to be a fun activity for the family, and just as fascinating for those without kids. Ideally, it can help inform what goes on that shopping list, and what perhaps shouldn't.

How to Do a Waste Audit

There are a couple of ways to do a waste audit for you, your family, or your housemates. Regardless of which method you choose, commit to auditing yourselves for at least two weeks. This will help you get a full picture of your habits and not just a snapshot.

The first method is simply to keep a log that gets marked each day with (1) each item that is thrown out, (2) the quantity of each item discarded, (3) the location (home or work) where it was disposed, (4) the reason it was tossed, and (5) the approximate value of what was thrown out (for example, if you bought yogurt for $3 and threw out a third of it, you'd enter $1). Do this only for waste that could have been edible. That is, only enter things that might have been eaten had they not spoiled, burned, molded, etc. Don't enter eggshells, chicken bones, or orange peels (but do check the Directory for great ideas on how to use those).

During your audit period, it's best to keep to your usual routine. Take this time to discover what you're wasting and why. There will be plenty of opportunity to improve later.

After the two weeks are over, look at which items come up most frequently, or which took the biggest toll on your wallet. Think of what you might have done differently to avoid tossing those items. That'll give you a good indication of where to start on your food-saving venture.

The second method, if you want to take it a step further, is to track specific quantities of discarded food, either by using a kitchen scale (and entering the weight in the quantity column) or by measuring weekly totals with a simple paper bag. For the paper bag method, mark a lunch-size paper bag with ¼, ½, ¾, and full marks at the start of each week. Line the bag with a regular plastic bag (or a compostable plastic bag if you're able to compost it at the end). Place all of your preventable food waste in there (again, no bones, eggshells, etc.), and clip the bag closed to reduce odors (keeping it in the freezer also helps). At the end of each week, note how high within the bag your waste reaches. After a couple weeks of this, try a few of the waste-reducing measures mentioned in this chapter and see if you can get the bag total down. How low can you go? Families might consider setting goals and offering children the approximate cash value of the food saved as a bonus to their allowance.

A Note on the Reasons for Discarding Food

Pinpointing the exact reason you're throwing food away is not as easy as it sounds. It actually requires a bit of reflection to do it correctly. For instance, let's say the lettuce in a bag of salad greens has gotten slimy. In the "Reason for Tossing" column, you could just enter "slimy," but is that really the reason? You could enter "didn't get to it in time," but even that's not really the reason. Take a moment to think back to what you had in mind when you purchased that bag of lettuce. Then think about what changed. Did you mean to bring salads for lunch, but then lacked the time to make them? Did you intend to eat it for dinner, but then went out with a friend instead or just popped a frozen pizza in the oven? Being as honest as possible about the root cause of the waste is the best way to diagnose how to reduce it.

You may have other reasons, but for starters, perhaps use the following categories:

- Bought too much

- Didn't cook as much as I thought I would (could also say "lazy/tired/busy")

- Didn't eat as much as I thought I would (could be "cooked too much")

- Weekly plans changed

- Didn't like

- Never felt like eating that food

- Didn't know how to cook

- Had to buy more than needed

- Didn't store it properly

Sample Weekly Wasted Food Form

	Food Thrown Out	How Much
Examples	*Broccoli* *Chicken stir-fry* *Turkey sandwich*	*½ head* *2 cups* *½*
Sunday		
Monday		
Tuesday		
Wednesday		
Thursday		
Friday		
Saturday		

What could you have done differently?

Where	Reason for Tossing	Estimated Value
Home	*Bought too much*	*$1.50*
Home	*Plans changed*	*$3.00*
Work	*Had to buy more than needed*	*$4.00*
		Total spent on wasted food

Smarter Storage

A good food-waste warrior is adept at storing food, but in fact the skill predates our civilization. Food storage is really an ancient art. Cave dwellers buried their hunted game in snow, and Inuits preserved seabirds in the hollowed-out belly of a seal. Storing food was a survival skill and also the inspiration behind all sorts of delicious traditional foods that we still enjoy today.

In this day and age, we have it pretty easy. What those cavemen wouldn't have given for a freezer! Still, storing your food properly is important to preserving its freshness and getting as much life out of it as possible. It can also be the difference between using it and losing it.

This chapter first lays out some basic principles of food storage. It's a precursor to the Directory in the last section of the book, which provides a food-by-food reference guide for storing and using up everything.

It also explores the refrigerator. You've likely used a refrigerator for most of your life, so you might think you've got that down. If so, can you explain why there's a cheese drawer? Which shelf is meat supposed to go on? In the "Demystify Your Refrigerator" text, I walk you through the details of how a refrigerator was designed to be used and the basics of keeping your food safe and fresh.

Freezing is a critical tool in food storage and is the subject of another section in this chapter. You probably know how to open your freezer and throw something into it, but the "Rely on Your Freezer" section gives some helpful tips for making sure the food is at its best when you thaw it out. For those of us who are organizationally challenged, the freezer can be a lifesaver in those moments when you realize you're just not going to get around to eating something in time.

The Food Storage Mission

Whether or not they knew it, those ancient cultures had found methods to slow bacterial growth and enzyme activity, as those are the two things that cause food to spoil. When microbes and enzymes are not active, your food lasts longer. So the basic tenet of food storage is: Stop microbe activity!

How? Well, microbes need moisture, warmth, time to grow, and, for some, oxygen. Taking these conditions away, even just one of them, will deter their progress. Much of this will already be second nature for you, but understanding the science behind some of the food storage methods you already practice will help you make smarter decisions from counter to refrigerator.

Moisture: Microbes need moisture. This explains why dried foods, such as pasta or rice, can last for such a long time. Using a dehydrator to dry fresh foods works to preserve them for this reason.

Warmth: Most microbes grow best between 41° and 135°F/5° and 57°C. Below that, their growth is slowed, and at freezing temperatures, it is stopped. Ensuring that your refrigerator is below 40°F/4°C is important to extend the life and enhance the safety of refrigerated foods.

Time: Microbes take time to grow and multiply. This is why being sure not to leave food at room temperature (or any temperature between 41° and 135°F/5° and 57°C) for any length of time is important.

Oxygen: Most microbes need oxygen to thrive. Decreasing exposure to air, such as through canning or even just using sealed containers to store your food, can slow decomposition and spoilage.

Low Acidity: High salt, high sugar, or high acid levels keep bacteria from growing, which is why salted meats, jam, and pickled vegetables developed as traditional preserved foods.

That's it. You're now an unofficial microbe expert and can explain why dried fruit lasts so long and why it's better to have storage containers that close completely. Keep these conditions in the back of your mind as you go about the business of running your kitchen. They may help you decide not only how to store food, but also whether it's safe to eat.

Demystify Your Refrigerator

You may think of your refrigerator as a place to display children's art, but the real art comes from using the refrigerator correctly. That means grappling with questions like, What's the deal with those adjustable knobs on the crisper drawers? Which foods belong on the top and which on the bottom? Why does cheese get its own drawer?

FOUR BRIGHT IDEAS

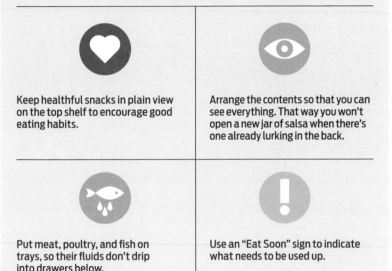

Keep healthful snacks in plain view on the top shelf to encourage good eating habits.

Arrange the contents so that you can see everything. That way you won't open a new jar of salsa when there's one already lurking in the back.

Put meat, poultry, and fish on trays, so their fluids don't drip into drawers below.

Use an "Eat Soon" sign to indicate what needs to be used up.

As you now know, one of the keys to slowing down the activity of bacteria and enzymes is temperature. The colder the temperature, the less active they'll be. Using the freezer stops them in their tracks.

The target number for your refrigerator is 40°F/4°C. If there is one thing you should remember from this entire chapter, it's to ensure that your refrigerator is at or below that temperature. If the refrigerator is too cold, delicate food like salads can freeze, and it will also use more electricity. If the temperature is too warm, the food can spoil more quickly or pose a health risk.

Some refrigerators have built-in thermometers, but most have a more ambiguous scale that goes from

Produce for High-Humidity and Low-Humidity Crisper Drawers

HIGH-HUMIDITY DRAWER

- Broccoli
- Brussels sprouts
- Carrots
- Cauliflower
- Green onions
- Leafy greens

CAN GO IN EITHER

- Citrus
- Melons (after ripe)

LOW-HUMIDITY DRAWER

- Apples
- Avocados (after ripe)
- Grapes
- Mushrooms
- Peaches (after ripe)
- Pears (after ripe)
- Peppers
- Squash

"cold" to "coldest." If yours does not have a thermometer, it's a good idea to go get one. They are well worth their low price, as they help you keep food at the right temperature and also identify when something is amiss with the refrigerator itself.

However, the temperature is not the same throughout your refrigerator. Since heat rises, a refrigerator is generally coldest at the bottom and gets warmer as you go up, with the warmest area being the door. Let's start from the top.

The **upper shelves** are warmer than those below, so use them for less risky items such as leftovers, drinks, yogurt, and snacks. It's also a good place to keep a bin or basket with small tidbits that might get lost elsewhere. I also keep a tray with an "Eat Soon" sign for things that need to be used up right away.

The **bottom shelf** is the coldest place in the refrigerator and is therefore best for meat, poultry, and fish. These foods have a higher safety risk, so they're better off kept colder. Storing them on a low shelf also reduces the risk of contamination if they leak.

Crisper drawers serve two functions. First, they create a different humidity zone than the rest of the refrigerator. Second, they allow different treatment of those products that could benefit from more airflow.

The best thing to do is to create a high-humidity drawer and a low-humidity drawer. If the drawers have levers, set one to high (closed, less air coming in, higher humidity) and one to low (open, more air coming in, lower humidity). If there are no levers, just crack one drawer open the tiniest bit, and that will be your low-humidity drawer.

Put fruits in the low-humidity drawer, along with vegetables that rot easily. Many fruits give off a gas called ethylene when they ripen, which speeds up the ripening of fruit next to it. That's fine if you're trying to ripen fruit (think peaches in a paper bag), but to make already ripe fruit last, you'll want the opposite effect. Storing fruits in the low-humidity drawer will allow more gas to escape.

Put most vegetables, particularly those likely to wilt, in the high-humidity drawer. The water in vegetables gives them their structure. When they dry out, they shrivel and droop, but with high humidity, they'll stay perky longer.

The **cheese drawer** is really designed to give your cheese a place to live without absorbing flavors from other food in the refrigerator, which cheese has a tendency to do.

The **refrigerator door** is the warmest part of the refrigerator, getting a nice dose of room-temperature air every time the door is opened. It's a good place for condiments. It is not a good place for anything that is even moderately perishable. Though some models may have a compartment for eggs in the door, it's better to keep them on one of the main shelves.

THE REFRIGERATOR DEMYSTIFIED

Stocking your fridge with these tips will help your food stay fresh the longest.

THE UPPER SHELVES

The upper shelves are slightly warmer than below, and are a great place to store items that don't have a high safety risk.

Great for leftovers, drinks, yogurt, dips, and sauces

THE LOWER SHELF

The bottom shelf is the coldest place in the fridge. Foods with a higher risk are better off in the coldest section.

Store meat, poultry, and fish here in trays to prevent them from dripping

HIGH- AND LOW-HUMIDITY DRAWERS

The adjustable levers on the crisper drawers change humidity levels. If your refrigerator has these, set one to high (closed, less air coming in) and one to low (open, more air coming in).

Put most veggies, particularly those that might wilt, in the high-humidity drawer.

Put fruits in the low-humidity drawer, along with vegetables that have a tendency to break down and rot.

Carrots, leafy greens, spinach, arugula, basil, broccoli, etc.

Pears, apples, grapes, mushrooms, peppers, avocados, etc.

COOL

COLD

Milk

DO NOT OVERFILL

The fridge needs air to circulate to be efficient. Allow enough space in between foods so that cold air can circulate all around.

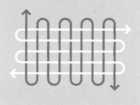

40° F/4° C OR BELOW

Because bacteria grow most rapidly between 40° and 140° F/4°C and 60° C, your fridge should be set to maintain a temperature of 40° F/4° C or below.

THE DOOR

The refrigerator door is the warmest part of the fridge, getting a nice dose of warm air every time the door is opened.

It's a good place for condiments. It is not a good place for anything that is even moderately perishable. Though some models may have a compartment for eggs in the door, it's probably a better idea to keep them on one of the main shelves.

NEVER LET ICE BUILD UP

It forces your fridge to use more energy.

WARMEST

Rely on Your Freezer

The freezer is the food-waste warrior's best friend. In the freezer, you can safely store food for long periods of time without feeling time pressure to eat it. Sure, you had the best intentions when you bought ingredients for that chicken parmesan meal, but somehow the week has gone awry and now the chicken has been in the refrigerator for a few days, uncooked. What do you do? Pop it in the freezer. That extra cooked pasta that you're not in the mood to eat tomorrow? Throw that in too. Going on vacation? Dump everything in the refrigerator into the freezer! Though some foods might change in texture, pretty much *anything* can be frozen. Seriously.

I've found from personal experience that if you're just going to throw something in for a couple of days, you don't really need to worry about how you freeze it (except for fresh fruits and vegetables, which usually require a quick blanch or purée). If you tend to forget what's in there, however, or are planning to leave it for longer, it's worth taking the time to do it right. There's no doubt that freezing in the right way can help improve food's quality when it's time to defrost.

The freezer can also allow a once-a-week cook to provide meals all week or even longer. Entire books have been written about freezing, in fact, with recipes and meal plans that can get you through a month with minimal cooking. Quality does deteriorate over time, though, so it's best to eat frozen food within a few months.

Generally speaking, if food has been thawed in the refrigerator, it's fine to refreeze it, even if not cooked, though the quality might suffer a bit. If it was frozen raw and then cooked, you can refreeze the cooked portion. Leftovers should be frozen within three to four days. If food has been out of the refrigerator for less than two hours, it's still okay to refreeze it. Beyond two hours outside of the refrigerator, meats, poultry, seafood, and dairy should not be refrozen. Rather, cook or reheat them first, and then freeze.[39] As noted in the thawing instructions, refreezing meats or seafood after thawing in water or in the microwave is not recommended unless they've been cooked.

Freezing is easy. The real challenge is remembering to use what you freeze! So many people "lose" things in the back of their freezer. One way to deal with this is to be well organized. Another, for less organized people like me, is to plan a "freezer night" every week or two so that you actually eat that container of beef stew before it is covered in ice crystals.

1. Prep

If you're just putting something in the freezer for a few days, you can probably skip most of these steps. But if you plan to store food for longer periods (or if that tends to become its fate regardless of what you plan), taking the time to prep it will result in a much better product at the other end.

Blanch vegetables and some fruits. Because blanching stops destructive enzymes in their tracks, produce that has been blanched is more likely to keep its quality, color, and vitamins. See the directions in the "How to Blanch" box on page 54.

Trim fat from meats and wrap well. The fattier the meat, the more likely it is to get rancid. So get rid of as much fat as you can. Do not freeze meat in its supermarket package (unless it comes frozen). Rather, wrap it as tightly as possible in either plastic wrap or freezer paper, pressing the wrapping right up against the surface of the meat. Next, wrap a layer of aluminum foil around the meat or seal it inside a zip-top freezer bag. The goal is to get out all the air to avoid freezer burn. If you get it directly from a butcher who has wrapped it, just put it in a zip-top freezer bag.

Separate moist items. To reduce clumping, spread moist items, such as berries, on a baking sheet in the freezer for about half an hour, then bag them up when frozen.

Purée watery items. Fruits and vegetables with high water content (such as tomatoes) can be puréed before freezing and later cooked in sauces or pie fillings, or used in smoothies.

→» How to Blanch

Vegetable Blanching Times

Blanching is recommended for nearly all vegetables before freezing because it stops enzyme activity, brightening color and helping slow loss of vitamins. It also softens vegetables, which makes them easier to pack.

Blanching is very easy and takes just a few minutes.

In a large pot, bring water to a boil—use 1 gl/3.8 L per 1 lb/455 g of vegetables.

If available, put the vegetables in a blanching basket (a strainer that fits into your pot).

Once the water is boiling rapidly, lower the vegetables into the pot, cover, and return to a boil. This should take only a minute (if longer, remove some water). Keep the heat on high for the entire blanching time.

Leave the vegetables in the water for the time shown in the "Vegetable Blanching Times" chart. Start counting the blanching time as soon as the water returns to a boil. Blanching time is important! Under-blanching may stimulate the activity of enzymes and maybe worse than no blanching. Overblanching causes loss of flavor, color, vitamins, and minerals.

When blanching time is up, immediately place the vegetables into a large quantity of cold or iced water, 60°F/15°C or below.

Note: Add 1 minute to all times if above 5,000 ft/1.5 km altitude.

Ranges apply to variations in thickness or size.

Vegetable	Blanching Time in minutes
Artichokes	7
Asparagus	3-4
Beans: Snap, green, wax	3
Broccoli (florets, 1½ in/4 cm across)	3
Brussels sprouts	3-5
Cabbage or bok choy (chopped or shredded)	1½
Carrots (diced or sliced)	2
Cauliflower (florets, 1 in/2.5 cm across)	3
Corn kernels	4
Greens: Young spinach	1
Most greens	2
Collard	3
Okra	3-4
Parsnips (diced or sliced)	2
Peas: sugar snap, snow pod	2½
Peppers, bell (strips)	2
Potatoes (diced)	3-5
Squash, summer (sliced)	3
Turnips (diced)	2

Source: Colorado State University Extension, "Freezing Vegetables," www.ext.colostate.edu/pubs/foodnut/09330.html.

2. Pack

Use clear, airtight containers. Push out as much air as you can and carefully seal, label, and date packages.

Divide into the right portions. Make individual portions. They defrost quicker and you'll have just what you need for an easy meal. Try this with bread (slice it first), meat (break a large pack of chicken breasts into two packs or form ground meat into individual burgers), or soup (use a muffin pan to freeze individual portions, then transfer to a zip-top freezer bag).

Form into stackable shapes. For example, you can put purées in freezer bags and freeze them flat.

Don't overload. Put in only as much food as will freeze within 24 hours (no more than 2 to 3 lb of food per cubic foot [150 to 230 g per liter capacity] of freezer space), and leave enough space for air to circulate around the packages.

Organize. Keep a kit nearby with labels and pens to mark the item's name and the date, and use a whiteboard or log to keep a list of what's inside. By keeping a record, you'll end up saving energy and avoiding freezer burn because you won't need to open the freezer as often.

→» What is Freezer Burn?

Freezer burn is caused by water molecules leaving the food and can result from temperature fluctuations during storage. It's harmless, so the food is safe to eat.

Still, since freezer burn can affect taste, we'd all rather avoid it. The best ways to minimize freezer burn are to avoid temperature fluctuations within your freezer (for example, make sure the door is kept closed and the freezer is well loaded) and to ensure that products are wrapped well in airtight packaging. Ice crystals inside a sealed package are normal. This simply means that moisture in the food and air inside the package has condensed.

PACKING THE FREEZER

KEEP ORGANIZED

Soup
3/15

Log

ALLOW FOR GOOD AIRFLOW

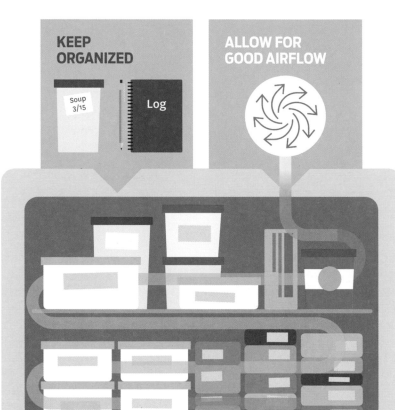

DIVIDE INTO THE RIGHT PORTIONS

FORM INTO STACKABLE SHAPES

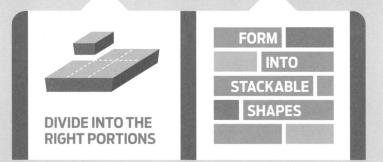

3. Thaw and Use

Use safe thawing methods. Thawing at room temperature gives microbes the time and temperature to thrive. Instead, thaw using one of these methods.

- *In the refrigerator:* Allow 24 hours to thaw most items in the refrigerator. Large items will need 24 hours for every 5 lb/2.3 kg of weight. Items will remain safe and good quality for a few days (one to two days for ground meat, stew meat, poultry, and seafood; three to five days for beef, pork or lamb roasts, chops, and steaks). Food thawed in the refrigerator can be refrozen without cooking, although there may be some loss of quality.

- *In water:* Make sure the item is in a leak-proof package. Place in a bowl of cold water and change the water every 30 minutes. Do not use hot water. It should take less than 1 hour for 1 lb/455 g to thaw; a 3- to 4-lb/1.4- to 1.8-kg package may take 2 to 3 hours. Foods thawed this way should be cooked immediately, and cooked before refreezing.

- *In the microwave:* Use the defrost option on your microwave to thaw foods. The time and power will vary by microwave. Cook food immediately after thawing, and cook before refreezing.[40]

Cook straight from frozen. Most vegetables and some other foods, such as sliced bread, do not need to be thawed before cooking. Meats can safely be cooked straight from frozen as well, but they may suffer in quality and will take about 50 percent longer to cook.

Add water. Sauces tend to thicken while they're in the freezer, so you may need to add water when reheating.

For the Slightly Audacious: Canning, Pickling, and Drying

For those wanting to put a bit more time and energy into storing food, traditional kitchen wisdom has a lot to offer. It may seem like the domain of country grandmothers, but canning and pickling are making a comeback. In fact, sales of home canning supplies rose by 35 percent from 2008 to 2011.[41, 42]

And for good reason. Preserving foods yourself is one of the best ways to stock your pantry with quality, wholesome products. Most of these techniques truly require only a bit more time and energy than freezing. They accommodate special diets, such as low sodium or low sugar, when such products can be hard to find commercially. They can make for thoughtful, inexpensive gifts. And because jars can be reused and only the lids need replacing, home canning vastly cuts down on the packaging waste (and footprint) of your kitchen. Plus, canning jars are glass, and therefore are not lined

with the chemical known as BPA (bisphenol A), which has been shown to have negative health effects. Be sure to buy jar lids that are BPA free.

Home preservation techniques are often used by gardeners who find themselves with a glut of a particular crop. Others like to take advantage of peak season and low prices at the farmers' markets or grocery store. In truth, however, you don't need all that much food to make some of these techniques worth your time. They can all be employed with quantities as small as a pint jar or a single tray.

Entire books have been written on food preservation techniques. Be sure to do a bit more research first if you plan to try them out, as some of the steps are quite important to the food's safety. An understanding of safe canning has evolved over the years, so while it may be tempting to use your great-aunt's recipe, be sure to read up on more current canning procedures as well. The National Center for Home Food Preservation offers an online course that will give you all the basics you need to know. Hopefuly I've whetted your appetite. Pickled green tomatoes, anyone?

Canning and Pickling

I can almost guarantee that the first time you can or pickle something, you will say to yourself, "I can't believe how easy that was!" I am by no means an avid food preserver, and I say that to myself pretty much every time I try it. A good way to break the ice is to find a few like-minded friends and make an evening of it.

Canning essentially involves cooking something, putting it in a jar, and then boiling the jar. There's really not much more to it than that. You do need to sterilize the jars and boil the lids beforehand.

You can cook foods to be canned in water, juice, syrup, or their own liquids, depending on the particular food. Sometimes you don't even need to cook it, but can just "raw pack" it into jars and then fill the jar with sugar syrup, juice, or vinegar brine. This works for berries, cherries, peaches, and anything getting pickled.

Canning vegetables and meats, which are less acidic, involves a somewhat more daunting process of pressure canning. I recommend starting with fruits or tomatoes that can be canned using the "boiling water bath" method.

Although there are a few pieces of specific equipment that make canning easier, you can get started with nothing more than a large pot and some canning jars, which you can purchase at your local hardware store, if not the supermarket. Of all the equipment, I find the jar lifter—special tongs that are designed for lifting jars—to be the one utensil that might be worth purchasing from the start. If you're hooked after you've tried it, you can then progress to more fancy equipment, such as special canning pots with racks, slicers, funnels, shaped spoons, and more.

Pickling is similar to canning and involves vinegar or salt brine. The acidity of the brine keeps the food from spoiling. There are several pickling methods, including fresh-packing, making chutneys and relishes, salt-brining, and freezing. A fermentation step can be involved as well. Fresh-packing can be as simple as placing chopped raw vegetables into a sterilized jar and pouring heated vinegar brine (typically vinegar, salt, water, and spices) into the jar. The jar then goes into a boiling water bath, as in canning.

Note: For safety reasons, when canning, it is important to follow a recipe from a trusted source. Do not eat any home-canned food that may be spoiled. If there is any bulging in the lid or odor or bubbling when you open the product, discard it.

Drying

Drying, or dehydrating, is just what it sounds like—removing the moisture from foods in order to preserve them longer (remember that moisture is one of the conditions microbes need in order to grow, and drying also slows food enzymes). Many foods were originally dried in the sun. While you can, of course, still do this, it is safer and faster to do so in either an oven or a dedicated food dehydrator. Because drying eliminates the water in foods, it makes them lighter, smaller, and easier to store.

In my opinion, a food dehydrator is one of the most fun kitchen toys around. Some dried foods can be eaten directly, such as dried fruits. You can make your own fruit leathers or vegetable leathers (why not?). Other foods are typically rehydrated before use. In fact, entire meals can be dehydrated and then rehydrated before eating. Think of camping meals. A friend of mine cooked and dehydrated an entire supply of meals for a four-month backpacking trip.

A food dehydrator is a small electrical appliance with heat, a fan, and vents for air circulation. Dehydrators are designed to dry foods fast at 140°F/60°C. They vary in size and features. Many are about the size of a microwave and have four to ten trays. There's a trade-off between being able to dry a good amount of food at once versus having to store a large appliance when you're not using it. A typical dehydrator with 9 square feet/ 0.8 square meters of drying space could dry about 28 bananas at once. Most people likely won't need much more than that.

The only downside to dehydrating foods is the time it takes (often 24 hours or more) and the energy (since heat has to be applied during the entire time period). If you live in an area with extended sunny periods, you can actually build your own solar dehydrator to cut down on energy requirements.

Root Cellars

Root cellars might bring up images of your grandmother's house or a tornado shelter somewhere in the Midwestern United States. But they're as useful and relevant today as ever. The general principle behind a root cellar is that some fruits and vegetables are best stored below room temperature but above the temperature of your refrigerator—at 50° to 55°F/10° to 13°C—and in a relatively humid environment. Fortunately, these conditions can be found by digging into the ground.

Root cellars are particularly handy for gardeners who have large quantities of foods that they're hoping can last much of the winter. Root vegetables, such as potatoes, carrots, and onions, do well in root cellars, as do squash, apples, and pears. Each food has particular details to follow when storing—some should be stored in sand, some covered with a damp towel. There are also combinations to avoid. For instance, onions placed near potatoes can cause the latter to sprout, and apples will turn nearby carrots bitter.

If you have some room in your basement or yard, consider buying a how-to-root-cellar book and learning about this traditional and useful technique.

The Crafty Kitchen

The kitchen is "Mission Control" for making the most of your food. It's where the magic happens: the slightly soft carrots are reborn as a rich carrot soup, the stale bread is transformed into the herbed crust of a fish fillet. It's also where less magic and more science happens if you're not careful.

Food-waste warriors approach the kitchen with a use-it-up mentality. They are ready to concoct new dishes that make use of whatever ingredients are on hand, not afraid to substitute pasta sauce or salsa in a recipe that calls for tomato paste. They shun tradition and eat breakfast for dinner, or dinner for breakfast, depending on what needs to be finished up. They occasionally resist the urge to go out to eat because they know there's a bunch of food in the refrigerator waiting to be cooked. They might even eat something they're not in the mood for.

It might sound unusual at first, but the use-it-up mentality can unleash a world of creativity. What do French toast, fried rice, and bread pudding have in common? They're part of a rich history in which different cultures have created ways to use up food that would otherwise be thrown away. It's not just Old World convention, though. It's likely that the use-it-up mentality is responsible for recipes that now adorn the plates of Michelin-rated restaurants around the globe. It's a state of mind that plays a regular role not just in restaurants, but also in helping me discover new dishes in my own kitchen.

You don't need any new tools or gadgets to incorporate a use-it-up mentality into your own cooking right now, but this chapter lays out some tips and strategies that can help. I should note, however, that the best practice is not to have surplus food in the first place. Toyota is known for its "just-in-time" manufacturing, which leads to minimal overage in its forecasting. The same principle is true for cooking; the less surplus, the better.

Set Your Kitchen Up Right

Spend a little time to make sure your kitchen is prepped and ready to be as waste free as possible. This means having the right equipment and foods on hand and creating a clean, welcoming space.

Above all, your kitchen should make you want to cook. You might already have a beautifully laid out, clean kitchen, but if your kitchen is cluttered and you can't easily find things, it might be subtly dissuading you from cooking the food you've already bought. You're unlikely to use items you can't see and have forgotten in the back of your pantry. You're likewise less likely to make a smoothie with that blackening banana if getting your blender involves a stepstool. If this rings true for you, start your journey to a waste free kitchen with a good cleaning and an organizational overhaul.

Organize

It's almost as though refrigerators were designed to hide food. Pantries are often not much better. The designers may have been trying to maximize food storage, but they certainly did not have optimizing the use of that food in mind. Nevertheless, most of us are stuck with the kitchens we have. Thoughtfully organizing your kitchen so that you can see as much as possible—and at least stay aware of the rest—is a fundamental step in using up all of your food.

The main goals are visibility and easy access. In cupboards and pantries, pull-out drawers or sliding shelves are the key to success. They make everything in the back of the cupboard just as visible and accessible as the items up front, eliminating the need to dig and restack.

In addition, organizers such as lazy Susans, baskets (wire baskets that you can see through are preferable), over-the-door organizers, drawer dividers, and lid racks can all help to increase the usability of everything in your kitchen. Simple trays can be used to increase cupboard space—just line them, put them atop glasses or cans, and put more items on top.

Labeling is useful too. For low drawers, label the tops of items. I like to keep food that I store in big containers, such as flour, grains, or beans, in those low drawers. In the higher cupboard drawers, I label the sides of items, if it's not something I immediately recognize.

Ensuring that you can see all the food in your refrigerator is not easy, so I recommend telling yourself what's in there instead. A magnetic whiteboard does the trick. Stick it on the refrigerator and update it every few days with leftovers and what needs to be used up. If you're really dedicated, you could do an entire inventory of what's inside. Either way, some sort of tally not only helps avoid food getting lost in the back, but also saves energy because you'll be opening the refrigerator door less. Don't want the list on the refrigerator door? Try painting the inside of a pantry door with chalkboard paint and keeping your running list there.

Kitchen Equipment

Gadgets that can help conserve food are not always specially designed for the cause, but rather are often common kitchen equipment used a bit differently. For instance, one of my favorite tools is a small muffin tin. I use it to freeze soups and cooked rice or beans in reasonable portions. Other items that might come in handy include the following.

Baking sheets, ice-cube trays, and muffin tins. These can all help you freeze items in manageable portions. Once frozen, you'll want to transfer them into zip-top freezer bags.

Baking spatula. Not the stiff flipping kind, but the flexible kind for scraping batter from the bowl when you make brownies. Why be restricted to baking? I use it for pretty much anything that's made in a bowl, food processor, or blender: salads, mashed potatoes, rice, smoothies—you name it.

Big soup pot. Since soups and stews are always a good way to make use of questionable produce and vegetable scraps, a big soup pot is a necessity for every food-waste warrior.

Clear storage containers. The clear part is a must, since it takes the mystery out of what's in the refrigerator. I use glass containers because they can go from the refrigerator to the freezer and then to the microwave (and sometimes the oven, depending on the type), and there's no risk of plastic leaching into the food. It's helpful if they stack well, particularly the ones you'll use for the freezer.

Pressure cooker. These are extremely handy to have around. They vastly shorten the time for cooking grains and beans, allowing you to eliminate a lot of cans and whip up a side to accent a meal without much planning.

Two large zip-top freezer bags. One "smoothie bag" for all your overripe fruits and another to save scraps for soup stock. More for freezing other items will be useful too. I reuse mine many times (though not with raw meat).

Bonus items:

Banana guard. Though not on the essentials list, I love these banana-shaped containers, mostly because they make me laugh, but also because they keep bananas from getting crushed when you take them on the go.

Canning equipment. Beware, canning can be addictive! If you're ready to take up a little pickling and preserving of your own, a minimal set of supplies—a pot with a canning rack, a jar lifter, and a metal canning funnel—are useful and often come in kits.

Dehydrator. These can convert many foods into their dried, and thus preserved, counterparts. They make fun toys, but there is a trade-off because they do use a lot of energy.

Produce life extenders. There are a variety of products out there that claim to help extend the shelf life of your produce. Some are herb-lined papers that get tossed into the produce drawer; others are machines that pump ozone into the refrigerator (which deters bacterial growth). They work to varying degrees. It certainly can't hurt to try.

Vacuum sealer. Vacuum sealing reduces freezer burn and the space food occupies, and, most important, extends shelf life by preventing air exposure. Be sure to use reusable vacuum seal bags to avoid unnecessary plastic waste. Vacuum sealing does not replace the need for refrigeration.

Foods to Have on Hand

Ironically, you need some foods on hand so that you're armed against wasting other foods. The staples listed here are key to the success of the use-it-up mentality. It's also good to stock some "hero" condiments that come to the rescue when a dish just isn't coming out right.

Basic cooking staples: Olive oil, high-heat oil (safflower, rice bran, or canola), sesame oil, vinegar (I always have cider, balsamic, and rice), soy sauce, mayonnaise, mustard, onions, garlic, canned diced tomatoes, honey, crushed chiles, and bay leaves (for soups).

Hero condiments that can improve flavor in a pinch: Maple syrup, hot sauce, barbecue sauce, lemon juice, soup bouillon, dried onions, Parmesan cheese, sun-dried tomatoes, raisins, almonds, and pickles.

Meal rounders that help complete a use-it-up meal: Eggs, at least one grain (rice, pasta, quinoa, and/or couscous), beans (either canned or dried, if you have a pressure cooker), frozen vegetables (I always have corn, peas, spinach, broccoli, and edamame), and either frozen meat, frozen fish fillets, or a package of tofu.

You might want to adjust this list according to your own taste and cooking style, but don't forget to replace these items when you see them running low, so you know there is always a meal to be made at home.

Tenets of Mindful Cooking

Here are a few basic waste-saving mantras to keep in mind as you go about your kitchen. They are simple, commonsense suggestions, many of which may already be part of your routine. Nevertheless, together they are the cornerstone of a use-it-up, surplus-free kitchen.

Use older stuff up first. When you're unpacking your groceries, rotate older items to the front and place the newest items in back (ideally, all would be visible). It may seem over the top, but using a small sticky sign that says "Eat Me First" has been shown to help.

Revive older food. Sometimes older food just needs a little injection of new life. For leftovers, this could mean making a new combination—for example, serving eggs with chili from a dinner earlier in the week or using leftover stir-fry as a salad topping. Add new spices to change up the flavor. Spread half-used dips on sandwiches. Soak wilted veggies in cold water to recrisp them. Toast crackers or tortillas for a couple minutes to un-stale them. (See more tips like these in the Directory.) If you question whether an item is still safe to eat, be sure to cook it thoroughly as opposed to using it raw (and see the next chapter, "Can I Eat It?" for more information on evaluating whether you can still eat something).

Try to use all parts of your food. Do you really use as much of your food as possible? Restaurants that cook nose to tail and root to stalk are popping up everywhere. Why not adopt that practice in your kitchen? The greens on top of beets can be used just like chard or eaten raw in salad. Stock can be made of bones, odd meat parts, and vegetable scraps. Even the way you cut and chop can make a difference. For instance, removing just the stem of a pepper instead of whacking off the whole top can gain you another two or three slices of pepper.

Notice what you throw out. The "Sage Shopping" chapter has instructions for conducting a waste audit, which sounds very formal but doesn't have to be. The idea is simply to take note of what you throw out most and why, so you can figure out where to target your waste-cutting efforts.

Keep a little notepad next to your garbage or compost and jot down each time you throw something away that could have been eaten (not peels or bones, just the milk or lettuce that went bad). Take a look at it after a few weeks, and perhaps buy smaller quantities the next time.

Freeze, freeze, freeze. Almost everything can be frozen without significantly compromising its nutritional value. Enough said. See the "Smarter Storage" chapter for instructions.

Make the Right Amount

Part of wasting less is cooking the right amount in the first place. If you're the type to cook once and eat leftovers all week—and you actually eat or freeze them—by all means do that. But if not, preparing too much food can lead to either eating or wasting too much food. This means that zeroing in on the right amount to cook can do good for both your waist and your waste.

What is the right amount? This, of course, depends on the amount you tend to eat. You probably have a system down for the things you cook most often, but for new items or larger groups, estimating can be a bit more difficult. Use the "How Much Should I Make?" table (facing page) to determine approximately how much to make. Take notes on whether these are the right quantities for you. Remember that for big dinners, you may not need full servings of every dish for every person.

How Much Should I Make?

Food	Amount per Adult	Amount per Child
Beef/pork/lamb (uncooked)	3 to 4 oz/85 to 115 g	2½ oz/70 g
Broccoli	Alone as a side: ½ head With other vegetables: 2 to 3 florets	1 to 2 florets
Chicken (uncooked)	About 5 oz/140 g	3½ oz/100 g
Eggs	2 eggs	½ to 1 egg
Fish (uncooked)	About 5 oz/140 g	3½ oz/100 g
Grains (quinoa, couscous, rice; uncooked)	¼ cup/60 g	2½ Tbsp
Lettuce, bagged	As side salad: 1 oz/30 g As entrée: 2 to 3 oz/60 to 85 g	Small handful Big handful
Lettuce, head	As side salad: 2 to 3 leaves As entrée: 4 to 5 leaves	1 leaf 2 to 3 leaves
Pasta (uncooked)	2 to 3 oz/60 to 85 g	½ to 1 oz/15 to 30 g
Pasta marinara sauce	⅓ cup/80 ml	2 to 3 Tbsp

Source: Derived from the Love Food Hate Waste portion planner, wales.lovefoodhatewaste.com/portions/everyday.

Salvaging Kitchen Crises

Uh-oh. The best-laid plans forgot to take into account the telephone call you got in the middle of cooking or the space-cadet move of adding a tablespoon of salt to a dish instead of a teaspoon. Sometimes a deep breath and a "c'est la vie" as you head for the compost is all you can do. But other times, a small rescue effort might make a difference and keep you from having to unnecessarily throw away food that can be saved. Here are a few tricks for making the best of a bad situation.[43]

Burned Food

Your best bet is to salvage the part of the dish that is not yet burned. Work quickly! For food burned on the stove top, remove the pot or pan from the heat immediately. Fill a wider pan with cold water and place the pot with the burned food in the water. Next, take a wooden spoon and remove the portion of the food that comes out easily. Don't scrape too hard or you'll take the burned part along with the food that's still good. For items burned in the oven, carefully skim the burned layer off the top.

If the food is cooked enough, taste it. If it has only a slightly burned taste, cover with a damp cloth and allow to sit for 10 minutes or so. If it still tastes burned after that, you have two choices: throw in some barbecue or hot sauce and name it "Smokey Sam's ___" or simply cut your losses and put that frozen pizza in the oven. Burned food can still be thrown in the compost, if that's an option for you.

Oversalted Food

There are three basic fixes for food that is too salty. Salt can often be rinsed off of vegetables, pasta, and even meat. For boiled foods, try boiling in new water without salt. Otherwise, submerge the item in a bowl of water for 5 to 10 minutes; much of the salt will dissolve into the water. For soups, stir-fries, or casseroles, try adding more ingredients (water, potatoes, more vegetables) to dilute the salty flavor, but be careful with ingredients such as broth and tomato sauces, which are often high in salt themselves. The other option is to offset the salt. Depending on the dish, try vinegar, lemon juice, or brown sugar. And next time, add salt little by little, tasting as you cook, as long as the food is cooked enough to be safely tasted.

Overcooked Food

Overcooked vegetables can be cooked a bit more and then either made into a puréed sauce or combined with some cream, stock, and spices to make a soup. I just douse overcooked pasta with sauce, but you could also make a variation on baked ziti by putting the pasta in an oven-safe dish, mixing sauce in, topping it with cheese, and baking it. Restore moisture to dry poultry by baking it at a low temperature (250°F/120°C) in a sauce that is one part broth and one part oil or butter. With other meats or fish, there's not much to do, other than adding some strong sauce or cooling it to use in a salad or tacos the following day.

Bland Food

The fix for bland food really depends on the food. Adding bouillon to the cooking water for rice and vegetables can help avoid bland flavors to begin with. Soups and stews often benefit from bouillon too, as well as from maple syrup. In fact, I add maple syrup to the most unusual dishes— stir-fries, beans, soups—and they're almost always the better for it. Hot sauce and barbecue sauce can help make all sorts of dishes more interesting. Then, of course, there's salt and other spices. And if it's just not working out, put on that use-it-up mentality and think about how to use the item as an ingredient in a different meal. Once I dumped some bland *pico de gallo* salsa made with tasteless tomatoes into a salad and added dressing. It worked out perfectly!

Love Your Leftovers

Leftovers conjure up an array of feelings. For some, cold Chinese food is the breakfast of champions. Others will go near food only on the day it's made. I'm certainly a leftover lover and advocate. Leftovers save me money, time, and food and can have more flavor a day or two after cooking.

I often hear people say something is not worth saving. If that's you, I encourage you to think about why you say it. Is it because there's not enough for a whole serving? Maybe it could make a good ingredient in something else. Is it because you won't eat it the next day? Then go back and read the "Make the Right Amount" section. And if it has to do with not wanting to get another container dirty, well, maybe you need to reboot your use-it-up mindset.

Assuming you are saving your leftovers, make sure you cool them promptly (a key safety tip, as mentioned in the next section). It can be handy to put leftover portions straight into lunch containers for the next day, or else label them with the date. I like to use a dry-erase pen so that I can reuse the containers. And don't forget to use those sealable, clear containers you invested in, so you can see what you have.

Keep It Safe

Large quantities of food are thrown out because people are worried it might make them sick. The next chapter, "Can I Eat It?," has more information on how food can make us sick, but arming yourself with the knowledge to keep a safe kitchen is one of the most important ways to reduce your risk. Kitchen staff in restaurants are trained on these same principles, and the U.S. Centers for Disease Control and Prevention (CDC) breaks them down this way for those of us at home: Clean, Separate, Cook, and Chill.[44] Follow these steps to protect yourself from illness.

Clean. Running a clean kitchen will get you started on the right foot. Rinse fresh fruits and vegetables in running tap water to remove visible dirt and grime (prewashed greens do not need rinsing). Wash your hands, utensils, and surfaces such as countertops and cutting boards with warm water and soap. Avoid bringing illness into the kitchen through your own sickness or acts such as changing a baby's diaper while preparing food (yes, the CDC actually lists that as a precaution).

Separate. Cross-contamination is a leading factor in foodborne illness. Cleaning before cooking will help avoid this, but also be keenly aware of what comes into contact with what. Separate raw meat, poultry, seafood, and eggs from other foods in your grocery shopping cart, your grocery bags, and your refrigerator. See "Demystify Your Refrigerator" on page 46 for information on where to put items in the refrigerator. When handling raw meat, poultry, seafood, and eggs, keep those foods and their juices away from "ready-to-eat" foods such as salads, cheeses, or anything that won't be cooked again. Put cooked meat on a clean platter, rather than back on the one that held the raw meat.

Cook. Thoroughly cooking food to a high enough temperature will ensure that harmful bacteria are killed. Use a food thermometer to measure the internal temperature of different foods to make sure you're cooking them sufficiently. Letting food stand for the specified period of time after cooking can also be important, because the cooking process continues even after the food is removed from the heat, raising the internal temperature of your dish. If using a microwave, be sure to stir and rotate food to avoid cold spots.

Chill. As described earlier, cold temperatures prevent most microbes from reproducing. Minimizing the time your food spends hanging out at room temperature is a key step to safe food. This means:

- *Refrigerating food promptly when you get it home from the store.* Two hours after leaving the store should be the max, one hour if it's hotter than 90°F/32°C.

- *Cooling leftovers quickly.* Put leftover food in shallow metal containers and/or use an ice water bath. Restaurant standards are to cool foods in less than six hours, getting them below 70°F/21°C in less than two hours.

- *Thawing and marinating foods on the bottom shelf in the refrigerator rather than on the counter.* Food can be thawed in cold water or in the microwave if it's going to be cooked immediately. See page 57 for more details on proper thawing techniques.

Foods to Be Particularly Careful With

According to the CDC, the following foods merit particular attention to following the Separate, Cook, and Chill steps just described:[45]

- *Raw foods of animal origin*—raw meat and poultry, raw eggs, unpasteurized milk, and raw shellfish.

- *Filter-feeding shellfish,* including mussels, oysters, clams, and scallops.

- *Foods that mingle the products of many individual animals,* such as bulk raw milk, pooled raw eggs, or ground beef (because a pathogen in just one animal could contaminate a whole batch). For instance, a single hamburger may contain meat from a batch of ground beef that mixed hundreds of source animals.

- *Raw fruits and vegetables.* Washing can decrease but not eliminate contamination. If it comes in a package, don't eat it raw after the date on the package—cook it instead if it's not spoiled.

- *Unpasteurized fruit juice.*

Party Hard, Waste Lite

Parties are a particularly important time to pay attention to just how much food is being planned. No one wants to run out of food at a party, but neither do you want to end up with bag after bag of tortilla chips going stale in the pantry. Here are a few things to consider when planning your next fiesta.

Make room. Your freezer will come in handy for party prep and leftover storage. So as your party nears, try to "eat down" your freezer to make room.

Plan. Even for the nonplanners among us, this is the time to break out a portion planner. Note, however, that most portion planners do not assume that there will be eight other dishes available in addition to the dish in question. Try entering only three-fourths of the actual number of people you expect. If it's a recipe you use often, make some notes for yourself after the party to remind yourself how appropriate your multiplication was.

The number of appetizers you serve depends on their type and the amount of other food you are offering. Their purpose is to make everyone feel welcome and comfortable, to take the edge off people's hunger when they first arrive, and to whet their appetite for any main dishes. Three or four bites of food per person should be plenty. For shrimp cocktail, oysters, or larger crostini, plan on about two pieces per person. If you're serving smaller single-bite hors d'oeuvres, allot three per person total. For a dip, 3 oz/85 g per guest will be plenty. Consider putting out some raw vegetables with your dip as a lighter, healthier predinner alternative to chips or crackers.

Precook. If you're not quite sure how much you'll need, try to precook some of your dishes and freeze them ahead of your party. When the big day comes, reheat in batches as needed. If you don't use it all, you can throw yourself a party for surviving your party.

Coordinate. Help your well-intentioned guests avoid feeling silly when they walk in with that third pasta salad that doesn't go with the Indian curry sitting next to it. First, when asking guests to bring food, start by providing a theme that gives them some culinary guidance. Then don't be afraid to give some more specific direction. In fact, get bold and assign! And just as with your own portion planning, tell them to cook for three-fourths of the guests you expect. Ask those who aren't big on cooking to bring the wine.

Containers. No matter how much you plan and coordinate, you're likely to have some food around at the end of the party. The cardinal rule is to have containers on hand so that you can send your guests home with "doggy bags." Old yogurt or takeout containers work great. If you only have your "good" containers to work with, it's up to you whether to risk sending them home with your friends. You can also include a note in your invitation asking guests to bring their own leftover containers. "Since I can't help but cook for an army, bring a container so you can take some bounty home." And if all else fails, most anything can make it home in a zip-top bag.

→ Holiday Hoorahs

Who doesn't love the holidays? Last holiday season, after sampling thirteen different cookies at a cookie swap one day, I headed for sweet potato latkes the next, followed by a Christmas Eve crabfest and White Russians made with homemade Kahlúa to ring in the New Year. While my stomach thoroughly enjoyed the whole eating marathon, my conscience knew how much of the food at those feasts wouldn't get eaten.

Wasting food is particularly ironic during the holiday season, when the food banks are overflowing with volunteers and the garbage cans are overflowing with wasted food. What typically happens on Thanksgiving strikes me as the ultimate irony; we feast to celebrate that our ancestors had enough food to survive their first winter, acknowledging that once upon a time food was something to be grateful for. Then the next day, we throw half of it away.

The U.S. Department of Agriculture (USDA) reports that 35 percent of the turkey meat sold to consumers in the United States does not get eaten (and that's not including bones). In comparison, only 15 percent of chicken meat is wasted.[46]

Why is so much more turkey wasted than chicken? "Possibly because turkey is more often eaten during holidays when consumers may tend to discard relatively more uneaten food than on other days," the USDA writes.

In fact, each year during Thanksgiving, Americans toss about $282 million of uneaten turkey into the trash. Along with the meat, that's equivalent to throwing out 105 billion gallons of water (enough to supply New York City for over 100 days) and greenhouse gas emissions equivalent to 800,000 car trips from New York to San Francisco. It's also enough turkey to provide each American household that is food insecure with more than eleven additional servings.[47]

As your holidays approach, be sure to keep party planning tips and other waste-reducing strategies in mind.

Party Portion Planning

	Per Person	Crowd of 25	Crowd of 50
Hors d'oeuvres preceding a full meal	2 to 3 pieces	50 to 75 pieces	100 to 150 pieces
Hors d'oeuvres without a meal (2-hour party)	5 to 6 pieces	125 to 150 pieces	250 to 300 pieces
Oysters, clams, and mussels (medium to large)	6 to 10 pieces	100 to 150 pieces	200 to 260 pieces
Shrimp (large, 16 to 20 per 1 lb/455 g)	5 to 7 shrimp	7 lb/3.1 kg	14 lb/6.4 kg
Casserole	–	Two or three 13-by-9-in/33-by-23-cm casseroles	Four to five 13-by-9-in/33-by-23-cm casseroles
Chopped meat for chili, stew, stroganoff, etc.	5 to 6 oz/140 to 170 g	7 lb/3.1 kg	12 lb/5.4 kg
Ground meat	1/3 lb/150 g	9 lb/4 kg	18 lb/8.2 kg
Poultry (boneless)	1/3 to 1/2 lb/150 to 225 g	10 lb/4.5 kg	20 lb/9 kg
Turkey (whole)	3/4 lb/340 g	18 to 20 lb/8.2 to 9 kg	35 to 40 lb/16 to 18 kg
Ribs: baby back ribs, pork spareribs, beef short ribs	3/4 to 1 lb/340 to 455 g	20 lb/9 kg	40 lb/18 kg
Roast beef or pork (boneless)	1/3 to 1/2 lb/150 to 225 g	10 lb/4.5 kg	20 lb/9 kg
Roast beef or pork (with bone)	3/4 to 1 lb/340 to 455 g	18 to 22 lb/8.2 to 10 kg	36 to 45 lb/16.3 to 20.4 kg
Steak (T-bone, porterhouse, rib-eye)	3/4 to 1 1/4 lb/340 to 570 g	20 lb/9 kg	40 lb/18 kg

	Per Person	Crowd of 25	Crowd of 50
Pasta (entrée)	4 to 5 oz/ 115 to 140 g	6 lb/2.7 kg	12 lb/5.4 kg
Pasta (side dish)	2 to 3 oz/ 55 to 85 g	3½ lb/1.6 kg	7 lb/3.1 kg
Rice and grains (cooked)	1½ oz/40 g	2 lb/910 g	4 lb/1.8 kg
Potatoes and yams	½ to 1 (medium)	6 lb/2.7 kg	12 lb/5.4 kg
Vegetable side dish	3 to 4 oz/ 85 to 115 g	4 lb/1.8 kg	8 lb/3.6 kg
Desserts served by the piece (brownies, bars, cookies)	1 or 2 pieces	30 to 36 pieces	66 to 72 pieces
Pan desserts (cakes, cobblers, etc.)	2-by-2-in/5-by-5-cm piece or 3-in/7.5-cm wedge	Two or three 9-in/23-cm round pans	Four or five 9-in/23-cm round pans
Ice cream, sorbet, or pudding	4 to 8 oz/ 120 to 240 ml	1 gl/3.8 L	2 gl/7.6 L
Drinks			
Soft drinks (8-oz/240-ml servings), punch (4-oz/ 120-ml servings)	1 serving per hour	25 servings per hour	50 servings per hour
Coffee (4-oz/120-ml servings) and tea (8-oz/ 240-ml servings)	1 serving per hour	25 servings per hour	50 servings per hour
Beer	1 to 2 bottles per hour	25 to 50 bottles per hour	50 to 100 bottles per hour
Wine	¼ bottle per hour	4 to 6 bottles per hour	9 to 12 bottles per hour

Sources: D. Simmons and C. Simmons, *Cooking for Crowds for Dummies* (Indianapolis, IN: Wiley, 2005); Food Network, "Thanksgiving Dinner Portion Planner," www.foodnetwork.com/holidays-and-parties/articles/thanksgiving-dinner-portion-planner.html.

Can I Eat It?

What if I told you that a good portion of the food in your trash didn't actually need to be thrown away? People often throw food out because they're afraid it will make them sick. The thing is, many people don't really understand how or why food makes them sick. This can lead them to inadvertently toss food that's perfectly good to eat. Conversely, it can also lead people to eat food that is potentially unsafe.

We are going to change all of that here. This chapter empowers you to decide for yourself if your food is still okay to eat, ultimately helping you to keep yourself, your family, and your dinner guests as safe as possible while also not throwing food away unnecessarily. It may feel a bit heavy on the science, but it's worth it for the perspective you will gain.

Let's start by drawing a very important distinction. Most food-borne illnesses come from food being *contaminated*, not from its natural process of *decomposition*. That is, something that is not supposed to be on the food accidentally gets onto it and ultimately makes you sick. That something is usually a microorganism of some kind, but it could also be a naturally produced toxin or an artificial chemical. Whatever it is, it typically finds its way onto food early in the food's life—on the farm or in the processing plant—though contamination can also happen in a restaurant or your home. But no matter where it happens, it's a whole different ball game than food spoilage.

Decomposition, on the other hand, is a natural process that starts the moment a fruit is harvested or a cow is milked. When food gets to the point that it tastes, smells, or looks bad enough that you don't want to eat it, it's "spoiled." But spoilage alone does not lead to foodborne illness. This doesn't mean you should eat rotten tomatoes, it's just clarifying that the spoilage process is not generally what makes you sick from food. See page 188 for more on where foodborne illness does come from.

A good food-waste warrior understands this distinction between contamination and decomposition. He or she also knows how to keep food safe and use it all the way up to the point when it's truly spoiled (and even sometimes beyond). This chapter covers information that will help you use your food for as long and as safely as possible.

Why Does Food Make People Sick?

If it's not sour milk that's making us sick, what is it? Most foodborne illnesses generally fall into two categories: (1) infections from living microorganisms or toxins produced by these organisms, or (2) poisoning caused by harmful toxins such as those of poisonous mushrooms or chemicals that have contaminated the food. Allergies can also cause illness, but as that's a bit of a different beast, I won't go into it here.

While our food's safety is still a big concern, we've come a long way. A century ago, typhoid fever, tuberculosis, and cholera were common foodborne diseases. Improvements in food safety, such as pasteurization of milk, safe canning, and disinfection of water supplies, have virtually eliminated those diseases. But as food is a living thing, knowing how to keep the food in your kitchen safe is a key skill of the food-waste warrior. See page 188 for a detailed description of why food makes you sick and how to keep a safe kitchen.

What Happens When Food Ages?

Wilting and softening are to veggies what wrinkles are to us—a normal sign of aging that isn't necessarily harmful. Understanding what's happening can help you evaluate whether or not the food is still usable and safe to eat. Warning: This may bring you back to your sixth-grade science project (in fact, if you happen to have a sixth-grader in the house, there are all sorts of great science projects based on what's discussed in this section).

From the moment it's harvested, extracted, or slaughtered, food begins a journey of decomposition. Natural enzymes in plants are still active after harvest and cause the color, flavor, and texture to change. Some products, such as corn and peas, will lose their sweetness. Broccoli will instead begin to toughen, and lettuce will lose water and become limp. Fruit may continue to ripen and get sweeter after harvest but will eventually begin to rot.

Different types of food age in their own ways. Fruit and vegetables are attacked by microbes. Bread typically dries out, though if moist it can harbor molds. Meat and seafood are mainly degraded by bacteria on their surfaces. Dairy products are unusual in that the bacteria that work in them can sometimes actually act to preserve rather than degrade them, though this may result in a change in flavor or texture.

In all of these cases, the activity of the enzymes and microbes is increased by warmer temperatures and access to oxygen—hence the general smart storage practices of placing foods in sealed packaging and refrigerating them.

Let's take a look at what is actually happening when we see common indications of aging, and whether they actually mean food has gone bad.

Generally Harmless

Browning on apples, bananas, and potatoes. The outer skin of these foods acts to protect the inside. When exposed to air, the inside "oxidizes" and turns brown. There's no harm in eating these foods if they are browned. Refrigeration and acidic solutions such as lemon juice can slow the browning a bit.

SAFE EATING

GENERALLY HARMLESS

- **Browning** (apples, bananas, avocados)
- **Bruises** (cut out bruises)
- **Curdled or sour milk** (if pasteurized)
- **Discolored greens**
- **Faded or darkened meat** (if it looks and smells okay)
- **Rotting** (cut out rotten parts)
- **Scars**
- **Staleness**
- **Wilting or wrinkling**

BETTER TO STEER CLEAR

- **Green potatoes**
- **Mold** (cut at least ½ in/12 mm off)
- **Rancid foods**

Bruising. Bruising is just what it sounds like—the result of a fruit or vegetable being bumped or squashed during its journey from the farm. These run-ins break down the cell structure, which leads to softening and brown coloring. Light bruising itself does not render foods inedible. However, bruised portions should be removed as they create openings for microbes.

Curdled or Sour Milk. As long as it's pasteurized (which almost all milk is), sour milk is not likely to make you ill (though the flavor may be off enough that you won't want to drink it). The smell test is a perfectly legitimate way to evaluate milk. As milk ages, it becomes more acidic, which creates an environment that is unfriendly to microbes that might cause illness. That acidity is also what causes milk to curdle—the same process that's done intentionally when making yogurt or sour cream. What this means is that you can still use milk that doesn't pass your sniff test in other ways, either to make your own homemade cheese or cream products or in baked goods (see the recipe for Sour Milk Pancakes on page 121). Mold on dairy products, however, is something to be more careful of, as discussed in the next section.

Important note: Unpasteurized milk is a different story, as it has not gone through the pasteurization process that kills many of the microbes. Food safety guidelines strongly recommend avoiding raw milk products due to their high potential to cause both food-borne illness and other disease. Anyone consuming these products should read up on the risks before hand.

Discoloring of lettuce leaves. Color changes or spots on lettuce do not indicate disease. Leaves might turn brown at the ends, a condition called "tip burn" related to a nutrient deficiency when the plant was grown. Brown spots and brown stains can result from exposure to too much oxygen or carbon dioxide. And lettuce can turn pink in the middle rib if exposed to higher temperatures. Lettuce with any of these imperfections can still be eaten safely, though you may want to remove the discolored parts for aesthetic reasons.

Fading or darkening of meat. The color pigments in meat naturally change color when exposed to either air or light. They usually go from purple-red in color to cherry red to a more brownish red. With ground meats, this might mean the meat on the outside of the package is bright red while the interior is still a purplish or grayish brown. This color change is normal and does not mean the product is spoiled. If accompanied by off-smells or slimy or sticky surfaces, however, don't eat the meat.[48]

Rotting. Vegetables tend to suffer from "soft rot," which is the result of bacteria attacking their tissue. While rotted vegetables are not something you'll want to eat, the bacteria involved are not the same ones as those that lead to food poisoning. Rotted portions should be removed, and parts that are not affected can still be eaten. Fruits, however, tend to be attacked more by yeasts and mold, which can be more toxic (see the next section, "Better to Steer Clear").[49]

Scarring. Scars are the result of a fruit's or vegetable's growth. For instance, if peaches are touching a limb when they grow, a scar will form there. Scars do not affect the edibility of produce, though scratches that happen later in a food's life can open it to invasion by microbes.

Staleness. Baked goods, chips, and crackers can become stale, which simply means the starches in the product are altering form and transferring moisture. It does not indicate a safety risk and fortunately can often be remedied by briefly toasting the item in the oven (even for crackers and chips).

Wilting (for example, greens and broccoli) and wrinkling (for example, peppers and tomatoes). These are both signs that produce has lost some of its moisture and therefore can't maintain its structure. Neither is an indication that the food will make you sick, and in fact they can often be reversed by a 5- to 10-minute ice water bath or by cooking.

Better to Steer Clear

Greening of potatoes. Green parts of potatoes, as well as sprouts and eyes, can contain natural toxins that are not destroyed by cooking. If a potato has turned a slight green color, it's probably best to discard it. The same goes for potatoes that taste bitter.

Mold. Mold is one of the things you want to watch out for. Although some kinds can be quite delightful, such as the mold that makes blue cheese blue, other types of molds produce toxins that can lead to foodborne illness, and that can't be "killed" through cooking. At times, the mold filaments, or roots, can reach 1 in/2.5 cm into a food, even if not visible. Though it's rare for a mold to be extremely toxic, it is advisable to discard foods that are overgrown with mold, or at least to cut off the moldy parts with a ½- to 1-in/12-mm to 2.5-cm margin.

Rancidity (oils/nuts) Perhaps you've used an old olive oil or eaten a nut that tasted completely and utterly disgusting. That item had likely become rancid. When fatty or oil-containing foods decompose, the result is often unpleasant odors or flavors. Light, air, moisture, and outside bacteria can hasten this process. Unsaturated fats are more prone to rancidity, which means that fish, poultry, and game birds will become rancid before meats that are higher in saturated fats, such as beef. Nuts, especially walnuts, pecans, cashews, and peanuts, are also high in unsaturated fats and therefore particularly susceptible. It's best to store any of these products at cool temperatures and in opaque and airtight containers or wrapping. (See the Directory for more specific storage suggestions.) Though they will rarely make you sick, rancid foods are something you're just plain not going to want to eat because of their bitter taste or off-smell.[50]

The Surprising Truth About Expiration Dates

Here's the deal: You know all those dates you see on food products, labeled "sell by," "use by," and "best before"? In the United States, generally speaking, they do not indicate the safety of your food, and they're often not regulated.

They don't even mean that the food is spoiled after that date. Typically, they are manufacturers' suggestions for when the food is freshest or at its peak quality. Many foods will stay good for days or even weeks after the date on the package.

Suggestions. For peak quality. That's all.

If this is news to you, you're not alone. Various surveys and studies show that between 50 and 90 percent of Americans misinterpret the date labels on food and are throwing food away prematurely.[51] It's no surprise that there's such confusion, as the dates are not federally regulated and are regulated at the state level inconsistently and intermittently. The only product for which "use by" dates are federally regulated is infant formula, and that's because nutrients decline over time, not because it would induce illness. Beyond that, some states regulate dates for some products, but generally it's left up to the manufacturer.

Understanding what these dates do and don't mean will help you waste less food.

While it appears that there is a rational, objective system behind the dates we see on our food, it's more arbitrary than that. Take orange juice, for instance. In most states, there are no laws requiring manufacturers to stamp a date on orange juice containers. It is up to up to the manu-facturers to figure the whole thing out on their own, by going through a series of decisions such as:

- Should the product have a date displayed at all? Supermarkets might demand this, but otherwise it's up to the manufacturer.

- Which words to use? Will it be "use by," "best before," "sell by," or "enjoy by"? It's up to the manufacturer.

- What does the date convey? Is it that the taste, or perhaps the color, might change a little? Or do they just want you to see it as a fresh product even if it will last quite a while longer? Since there's no official definition, a range of factors can feed into what the date actually means.

- How is the date calculated? The manufacturer might use lab tests, do consumer taste tests, or look at literature values or just sales data. Anything goes here.

You might think that there is similarity in the dates, at least across orange juice brands, so that when you're looking at two containers of orange juice, the dates are compa-rable. Nope. Not the case. Go into a store and check out the orange juice lineup, and you'll see for yourself.

There are a few foods for which it does, in fact, make sense to heed expiration dates. These are foods that carry a high risk of a particular patho-gen called *Listeria monocytogenes*, and they include deli meats, unpas-teurized cheeses, smoked seafood, and any premade sandwiches with these ingredients. See Foodborne Illnes (page 188) for more details.

The bottom line is that a food that is past its date is not necessarily bad. Nothing can fully guarantee that a food is safe, but using your judgment, your knowledge of why food goes bad and what leads to foodborne illness, and your safe food-handling practices are the best ways to protect yourself from contaminated food and from wasting it unnecessarily.

DECIPHERING THE DATES ON PRODUCTS

Some products don't have any words to explain the date. In those cases, how are you to know whether the date is telling the store to sell it by then or telling you it is at its best quality until then?

There is not a legal definition for this phrase in most states, and it is almost never legally distinguished from "best before" or even "sell by."

The only products for which this phrase is federally regulated is infant formula, and that's because the nutrients decline, not because it spoils.

Use by
Oct 20

This is typically used to indicate the "manufacturer suggestion for peak quality" of the product, not the food's safety.

Twenty states restrict stores from selling products after these dates; thirty states don't. Are people in those twenty states better off?

Some nonperishable foods have a date even though they'll be fine long after. Think of a box of mac 'n' cheese.

Several different methods could have been used to determine this date, from lab tests to consumer satisfaction assessments. There's no way for you to tell which method was used.

Source: Natural Resources Defense Council

Hey You: Be Careful!

Not all of us respond equally to the microbes and toxins that lead to foodborne illness, and certain people are more susceptible than others to health risks. Those who are more likely to be affected by risky foods should take more precautions, particularly when it comes to unpasteurized dairy or ready-to-eat foods. Higher-risk populations include the following groups.[52]

Infants and toddlers. Babies' immune systems are still developing. As well as practicing the usual precautions, consult a doctor on particular foods to avoid to protect against foodborne illnesses.

People with compromised immune systems. Chronic illnesses, including HIV/AIDS, cancer, and diabetes, can weaken immune systems, as can some of the treatments associated with these diseases. This is true for transplant recipients due to the medication they take. People with these medical conditions should consult their doctor on the appropriate precautions to take with their food.

Pregnant women. Pregnancy hormones weaken a woman's immune system, reducing her ability to fight off harmful organisms. Furthermore, an unborn baby's immune system is not fully developed, putting the baby at risk as well. *Listeria* (see the box on page 189) is of particular concern, as it can pass through the placenta to an unborn baby without the mother showing signs of illness, leading to serious and even fatal consequences for the embryo. Pregnant women should thus be extremely careful with foods that have a risk of carrying *Listeria*, such as deli meats, ready-to-eat sandwiches, unpasteurized soft cheeses, and smoked seafood. The Centers for Disease Control and Prevention provides detailed guidance for smart dietary choices during pregnancy.

Older adults. People's immune systems weaken with age. This means they are less likely to fight off a foodborne illness and also may suffer more severe consequences if they contract one. The U.S. FDA cites seventy-five years of age as the point at which the risk of foodborne illness increases.

Getting Scrappy

By now, you're a food-waste warrior black belt and are probably down to discarding mere scraps in your kitchen. But no matter how methodical you've been in planning, cooking, and eating the food you've purchased, peels, pits, and bones will always be there, as will the occasional container of too-old-even-for-a-food-waste-warrior food. Not to worry.

Doing something other than sending these supposedly unusable food scraps to a landfill is the name of the next game—one that can provide some fun activities for you, your family, and even your dog.

Think back to the food recovery pyramid at the beginning of the book that provided a framework for putting food to its highest and best use. It tells us that in our homes, after feeding people, the highest and best use for food is to feed animals. Next on the pyramid, after industrial uses, is composting or putting it through a garbage disposal.

If you have food that is simply extra—perhaps you're cleaning out your pantry or hosting an event—consider contacting your local food bank for suggestions on who might be able to accept it as a donation. Not all food banks are able to accept small quantities, but they will likely know a church, soup kitchen, or other location that would happily use it to help feed those in need.

This chapter, however, is not about food that can be donated. It's about scraps. I'll map out all of the amazing things you can do with those scraps you previously regarded as trash. You'll learn about a number of surprisingly fun and creative projects you can try out to put those scraps to use, what scraps you can feed to your animals, and the magic and practicalities of composting. Let's put it this way, by the end of this chapter, you'll never look at an avocado skin the same way again.

Food Scraps for Your Pets

Pet owners vary in their approach to feeding their beloved furry ones. My grandmother used to buy a whole chicken and make her dog fresh chicken soup daily—no kidding! I know others who feed strictly dog food and nothing else. I fall squarely in the middle of the spectrum. It's mostly dry food for my pup Tulsa, but every so often, when something falls on the floor or she's otherwise lucky, she does score some "people food."

According to the food recovery hierarchy, if something can be fed to a pet, that's a higher use than throwing it out or even composting it. So I'm okay with that approach. Plus, what might be garbage to you and me can be a gourmet meal for your dog.

That said, I've often wondered what's actually safe to feed Tulsa. There are so many rumors out there. It's not a problem exclusive to dog owners; cat owners confront the same question. To help with all the confusion, here are some things to keep in mind when tossing scraps to your pets.

Foods to Avoid for Cats and Dogs

Dogs, and perhaps some cats, will eat almost anything you put in front of them. For that reason, it's easy to think of them as garbage disposals on four legs. But our pets' digestive systems are more sensitive to the quality and quantity of the people food they eat than we tend to realize. It's not that you can't give them scraps; you just have to be discerning.

Scraps should be considered treats rather than full meals. The general rule is that no more than 5 percent of your pet's diet should come from treats or people food, to make sure your pet gets the balanced diet he or she needs, which commercially sold pet foods are designed to provide.[53]

While dogs and cats have different dietary needs, many of the same foods can cause them harm. Avoid feeding your pets anything too oily, saucy, or spicy as it could wreak havoc on their digestion. Bear in mind, too, that our pets can develop heart disease and diabetes just as we humans can, so avoid feeding them too many foods laden with sugar and fats. In fact, cats supposedly can't even taste sugar!

DO'S AND DON'TS FOR FEEDING SCRAPS TO DOGS AND CATS

SAFE
FOODS TO FEED YOUR PET

- Cooked meat and eggs
- Fruits and vegetables (except those listed to the right)
- Oatmeal
- Peanut butter
- Rice
- Salmon and fish skins

HARMFUL
FOODS TO AVOID FEEDING YOUR PET

- Alcohol
- Avocado (can cause indigestion)
- Bread dough (active yeast can cause severe effects)
- Caffeine, including coffee and caffeinated sodas
- Chocolate, especially dark chocolate
- Cooked bones (can splinter and cause internal punctures)
- Fatty and fried foods
- Grapes and raisins (can cause kidney failure)
- Hops from brewing
- Ice cubes (can crack their teeth)
- Macadamia nuts (can cause weakness and tremors)
- Moldy foods
- Onions, garlic, and shallots in large amounts—small amounts used in cooking are fine
- Raw fish (cats only—can prevent them from absorbing important vitamins)
- Sugar-free foods with the ingredient xylitol

Sources: ASPCA, "Foods That Are Hazardous to Dogs," www.aspca.org/pet-care/virtual-pet-behaviorist/dog-behavior/foods-are-hazardous-dogs. American Veterinary Medical Association, "7 Foods You Should Avoid Feeding Your Dog or Cat," www.avma.org/public/PetCare/Pages/foods-to-avoid.aspx.

On Raw Meat and Bones

Whether raw meat and bones can be fed to cats and dogs is heavily disputed. It's worth understanding the risks before making up your own mind.

Cats and dogs can digest raw meat, so it's not an issue of nutrition or toxins. However, just as for humans, raw meat carries the risk of contamination by *Salmonella* and other pathogens. While dogs and cats often pass *Salmonella* through their bodies without showing any symptoms of food poisoning,[54] the U.S. FDA recommends cooking meat thoroughly before feeding it to animals in order to kill any bacteria that might be on it.

For bones, the arguments are slightly different. There seems to be agreement that cooked bones splinter more easily than raw ones and thus carry more risk of causing an internal puncture if swallowed. Advice ranges from not feeding cooked bones to your pet at all to supervising their consumption carefully. Raw bones are said to be an excellent source of calcium and phosphorus, and possibly help pet tooth health. However, they may not be readily digested and still have some risk of splintering.[55] Also, the larger the bone, the less likely it is to splinter, so beef knuckles are safer than chicken neck bones. Splintering is a greater risk for dogs than for cats, as their jaws are much stronger.

Have You Heard? Backyard Chickens Are All the Rage

In my twenties, I had three hens in my tiny backyard in Portland, Oregon. It was the best. Not only did they lay fresh, delicious eggs almost daily, but they also kept weeds down and ate all of our fruit and vegetable scraps. Some people also enjoy having their children see firsthand where their eggs are coming from. Lately, the trend of raising chickens in backyards has been growing fast. Cities and states across the country have been revising their laws to allow for it, and residents are responding. One website that gives advice on raising backyard chickens has more than 125,000 members,[56] and there's even a dedicated magazine called *Backyard Poultry* with more than 75,000 subscribers.

DO'S AND DON'TS FOR FEEDING SCRAPS TO CHICKENS

If you have chickens, you probably already know what they can and can't be fed. For those considering jumping on the bandwagon, here's a quick roundup of how much of your own food scraps could be going toward making fresh eggs for you.

SAFE
FOODS TO FEED CHICKENS

- Cereals
- Cheese
- Fish and seafood
  (cooked)
- Fresh flowers
- Fruits and vegetables
  (virtually any, except those
  listed to the right)
- Grains, cooked
  (pasta, oatmeal, rice)
- Yogurt

HARMFUL
FOODS TO AVOID FEEDING CHICKENS

- Anything too salty
- Avocado
- Candy, chocolate, sugar
- Citrus
- Dried or undercooked beans
- Raw eggs or eggshells
- Raw green potato peels

From Garbage to Garden

Perhaps you've seen the classic windowsill experiment in which an avocado pit, set in a glass of water and supported by toothpicks, begins to grow roots. Avocados are one of many plants that can regenerate right in your kitchen. Some can produce decorative houseplants, some make for a good science experiment, and others can even produce another crop of vegetables. Here are more ways to complete the cycle of life for your food scraps instead of tossing them.

Celery, bok choy, and green onions. These vegetables can actually regrow themselves from their scraps. For celery and bok choy, cut off the bottom 1 in/2.5 cm of the bunch and put it in a bowl with the cut side up. Add just enough water to reach the bottom of the plant, and place in a sunny spot. A few days later, when roots have formed, transfer it to your garden or a pot with soil and watch your plant grow new stalks! If you remove just a few stalks at a time, they will continue to grow back again and again. Green onions are similar but can be placed directly in the soil. Make sure to bury the white bulb.

Citrus seeds. Take the seeds from that delicious orange or lemon and grow a whole new tree with them. Just rinse the seeds in warm water and soak overnight. Plant your soaked seeds in potting soil about ½ in/12 mm deep and 1 in/2.5 cm apart, then place in a warm, sunny spot and water regularly. In about one month's time, sprouts should start to appear.

Pineapples. That green hairdo on top of your pineapple can turn into a lovely houseplant. Cut off the pineapple crown where it meets the fruit, making sure no fruit is left on it. Peel off a few of the bottom leaves and place the remaining crown in a narrow jar with enough water to cover the bottom. Roots should appear in two to three weeks, at which point you can transfer the plant to a pot, burying at least 1 in/2.5 cm of the crown. Place the pot in a warm, sunny spot. Though unlikely to bear fruit, it may produce a pretty blue flower.

Potatoes and sweet potatoes. Have a little chunk of potato that you're not going to use? It only takes about a 1-in/2.5-cm chunk to start a new potato plant. You can also use a potato that has started to grow sprouts (which might be a good idea, as any potatoes that have a green tint to their skin are no longer suitable for eating). Cut whole potatoes into chunks, or use a scrap chunk, as long as it has at least one eye (the part of the potato where sprouts come out). Allow the chunks to dry out for one to two days, and then plant them in soil with the eyes facing up.

Root vegetables. Use the tops of carrots, beets, turnips, or radishes to get a nice table centerpiece. Fill a pie plate with about 1 in/2.5 cm of pebbles, leaving another 1 in/2.5 cm of room at the top. Arrange the vegetable tops on the pebbles so that they stand up straight, using some of the pebbles to keep them in place. Add water until it covers the bottom of the vegetable pieces. As long as they are touching water, the tops should sprout in about a week. Your new plant arrangement will provide a nice centerpiece that will last about a month.

Tomato, pepper, cucumber, zucchini, and squash seeds. Sometimes you taste the most delicious tomato and wish you could have it again. Well, you can at least try by saving the seeds and planting them the following gardening season. Each of these vegetables has a slightly different process for capturing and saving seeds that generally involves washing or scrubbing off pulp (if necessary), then drying the seeds on a paper towel or newspaper and saving them in a cool, dark, dry place. For tomatoes, experts suggest fermenting the seeds in their own juice for a few days before washing and drying. Research the method before saving the seeds, either online or in seed germination books, so that you have the best chance of the seeds growing into fruiting garden plants.

Household Uses for Food Scraps

Sure, you think food belongs in the kitchen. However, food scraps can have uses all over the house. Many of the natural cleaning products sold in stores are based on food plants and use some of the home cleaning remedies described in this section. They may not always be as effective as their chemical counterparts, but there are plenty of good reasons to reduce our exposure to chemicals in the home. Give some of these a try and decide for yourself.

Avocado planters or bowls. Use the halved skins of avocados to make cute little planters for any seedlings you're starting to grow. They're also a great way to present dips on an appetizer plate. Who needs bowls?

Banana-peel shoe polish. It may seem odd, but banana peels can make your loafers or pumps look spiffy. Simply rub your shoes with the insides of your banana peels, then give them another rubdown with a clean cloth. It's pretty neat how well this works.

Citrus metal polish. There's a good reason why you see so many citrus-scented cleaning products on your supermarket shelves; a little citrus goes a long way when it comes to removing stains, especially from metal. Simply sprinkle some baking soda and/or salt on the inside of any citrus fruit and get to work on brass and copper. Don't use on stainless steel, as it could scratch it.[57]

Coffee facial scrub. If your skin could use a revitalizing kick, used coffee grounds are the perfect way to do it. It sounds awkward, but the results will speak for themselves. Mix together three parts finely ground coffee to two parts olive oil (you should get two to three uses per 1 Tbsp of coffee). Though the result may look like mud, it will bring a new luster to your skin. To use, gently rub a small dollop of the mixture on your skin and rinse with water. Your new scrub will last several weeks at room temperature and even longer in the fridge.

Easter egg dye. Why buy synthetic dyes at Easter time when you can get vibrant colors from a few things around the kitchen? Scraps from purple cabbage and beets and peels from yellow onions can all be boiled

EASTER EGG DIY

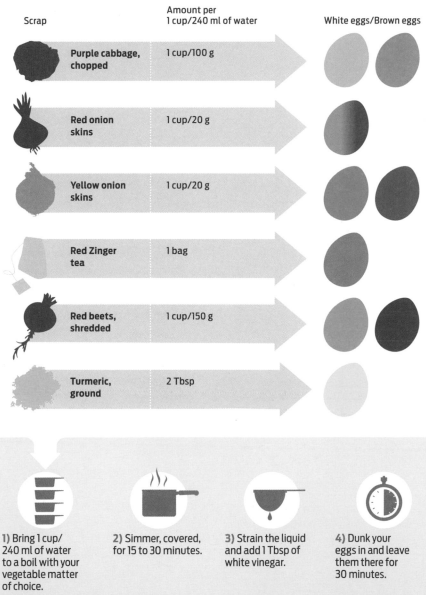

Scrap	Amount per 1 cup/240 ml of water	White eggs/Brown eggs
Purple cabbage, chopped	1 cup/100 g	
Red onion skins	1 cup/20 g	
Yellow onion skins	1 cup/20 g	
Red Zinger tea	1 bag	
Red beets, shredded	1 cup/150 g	
Turmeric, ground	2 Tbsp	

1) Bring 1 cup/ 240 ml of water to a boil with your vegetable matter of choice.

2) Simmer, covered, for 15 to 30 minutes.

3) Strain the liquid and add 1 Tbsp of white vinegar.

4) Dunk your eggs in and leave them there for 30 minutes.

down to create eye-catching dyes for your Easter eggs. For each color, bring 1 cup/240 ml of water to a boil with your choice of vegetable matter (see the list on page 103), then simmer, covered, for 15 to 30 minutes. Strain the liquid and add 1 Tbsp of white vinegar. Dunk your eggs in and leave them there for 30 minutes. You'll have perfectly dyed eggs, as pretty as anything you could have made with dye bought from the store. A total of about 4 cups/960 ml of dye is needed to color one dozen eggs.

Eggshell garden supplement. Crushing up eggshells and digging them into the soil is a great way to enrich your garden with much-needed calcium. They also keep away the slugs and snails that might easily feast on your flowers and plants. Briefly boiling the shells first will eliminate any risk of introducing pathogens.

Composting

In nature, there is no waste. Picture a lush rain forest. Amidst all the dramatic colors, spoiled fruit and dead leaves are constantly falling to the jungle floor. Are these wasted? Absolutely not. Once those fruits and leaves hit the ground, microorganisms and creatures such as worms get to work breaking them down into their valuable nutrients and slowly but surely incorporate them into the soil, where other plants use those nutrients to grow anew.

Your kitchen may not be as exotic as the Amazon, but when you compost, you're putting this same principle into action. Apple cores and potato skins break down into a soil dense with nutrients. Clipped grass, old flowers, dropped leaves, paper towels, and even paper plates will compost as well. After a compost pile has been left for a while, the result is a rich, natural fertilizer that can be used by other plants to start the cycle all over again.

Composting has the edge over the garbage can for two main reasons. First, it combats climate change by preventing food scraps from going to a landfill, where they produce the powerful greenhouse gas methane as they decompose. Food is the largest contributor to landfills today in the United States, and less than 5 percent of all food waste is composted. Composting food instead of sending it to a landfill is a simple way to reduce your carbon footprint, since as long as compost has enough air, it produces less greenhouse gas than food in a landfill.

Second, composting recycles your food. When a food is harvested, the nutrients in it are taken off the land and out of the soil. Composting turns your food scraps back into available nutrients, creating fertilizer that can be used to feed new plants. This has a further bonus of reducing climate change, as it offsets the need to use artificial fertilizer (which creates significant greenhouse gases as part of its production and use). In addition, when used as a natural fertilizer, compost improves the soil quality and releases nutrients in a slower, steadier way.

Using compost for growing food has a host of other benefits for gardeners and farmers. It can save water by helping the soil hold moisture; it protects plants from droughts and freezes, and reduces weeds when used as a mulch; and it adds beneficial microbes to the soil and attracts root-friendly organisms such as earthworms. The list goes on and on.

What does this mean for you? If possible, compost those scraps! If you have a backyard, you can start your very own compost pile there. If you're fortunate enough to live in a community that offers curbside food-waste collection, all that's required is throwing your food scraps in a separate bin from your other trash. Even those in high-rise apartments have options for composting. All you need to know to get started is covered right here, completing your road to a waste free kitchen.

Backyard Composting

Composting is easy. Follow these steps and you'll be at it in no time. Once you get started, you'll be amazed at how many scraps your compost pile can process and how much less garbage you'll have.

Set Up Your Compost Bin (or Pile).

First, choose where your compost will live. Look for a spot about 3 by 3 ft/ 1 by 1 m that's mostly shady and is reachable by a water source. Allow a minimum of 2 ft/0.6 m from your house or any other structure, such as a fence. If done right, compost piles should not have any odor associated with them, but just in case, you may want to locate it a short distance from your house, if possible.

Next, decide if you'd like to buy a bin or just create a compost pile. While bins are not absolutely necessary, they do make the process neater, prevent wind from blowing things around, and help prevent critters such as raccoons and opossums—and even your own pets—from scrounging around.

A compost bin should be about 3 ft/1 m in diameter and preferably not taller than your waist (for easy turning later). It doesn't have to be elaborate. If you're handy, you can easily build such a bin with pieces of scrap wood or just a few supplies. Otherwise, ready-made compost bins are often sold at hardware or gardening stores (or online). Something simple and inexpensive will do just fine. If you want to get fancy right off the bat, go for one that rotates or "tumbles"—these make turning your compost as easy as turning a knob. If you think you'll generate more food and yard scraps than a 3-by-3-ft/ 1-by-1-m bin can process, you can add more bins (or create your own partitioned structure where the contents of one part can be left to break down while you're filling up another part).

Collect Scraps. To begin your composting adventure, you'll need to start collecting all those food scraps you'd usually throw in the garbage. Place a small container under your sink or in another convenient kitchen location. An old pot will do, but nowadays you can also find sleek-looking compost containers for your countertop with filters that help to control odors. Compost bins can even be inset into countertops. You may also choose to line your container with compostable bags. Although these do make the whole process less messy, they are not necessary. In addition, they are not likely to break down in your backyard bin. Rather, they are designed to be composted in a commercial environment. Another option is to store your scraps in a plastic bag in your freezer until you're ready to bring them to the compost, which helps keep the "ick" factor down significantly.

You'll also need to learn the rules of what can and can't go in your compost bin. The main rule you need to observe is that anything you add to your compost pile must be plant matter. Dairy or animal products won't do for a household compost bin, as composting them safely requires much higher temperatures than those reached by your small backyard pile. (If your city collects food waste, it should be able to take dairy and animal products, as its piles will be much, much bigger and hotter.)

Start Composting. Composting is all about balancing "greens" (such as fruits and vegetables) and "browns" (such as wood shavings and dry leaves) with the right amounts of air and moisture. The greens provide nitrogen and the browns provide carbon—and if the mix is not right, odors result. Done correctly, your compost should smell like nothing other than earthy dirt.

Begin by layering the bottom of your bin with brown matter, anything from dead leaves and branches to

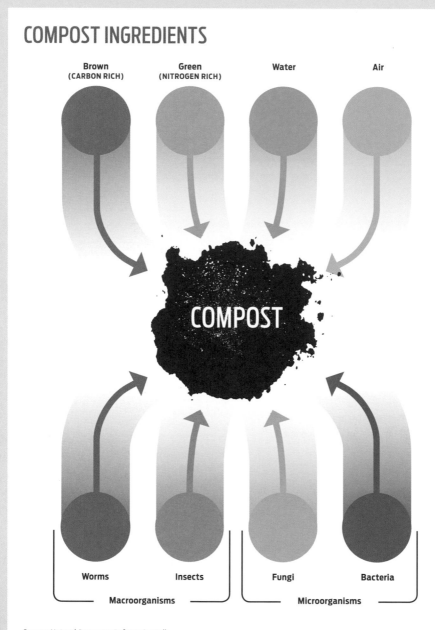

COMPOST INGREDIENTS

Brown (CARBON RICH)

Green (NITROGEN RICH)

Water

Air

COMPOST

Worms

Insects

Macroorganisms

Fungi

Bacteria

Microorganisms

Source: Natural Resources Defense Council

shredded newspapers and cardboard. If you have tree branches or other matter that's thicker than a finger, you may need to chop or break those pieces to ensure that they're small enough to let air circulate in your pile. This layer will help your food scraps decompose and reduce any nasty smells you may be worried about.

Next, layer your food scraps and fresh yard clippings (if you have them) on top of the brown matter. The best proportion is roughly two parts brown to one part green. Every few days, take your food scraps and toss them onto the pile, adding more brown matter and a thin layer of soil on top each time. Think of it as an earthy lasagna or tiramisu! Turn this mixture over with a shovel or garden fork (or, if you've sprung for the fancy rotating bin, just spin it) once every week or two. Also, make sure the mixture stays damp by sprinkling it with water every now and then (unless your food scraps are moist enough to keep the pile going).

Over the next few weeks, you'll see your old food scraps break down into dark, earthy, soil-like matter. If your pile isn't doing anything, make sure you're adding enough nitrogen-rich material (greens) and that it's moist enough (like a wrung-out sponge). If your pile is smelly and wet, add more browns and turn it more frequently (and make sure the materials you're adding aren't too big and preventing airflow).

Using this basic recipe, you can have a bin full of compost in less than two months.

Make Good Use of Your New, Rich Fertilizer! Once your compost is ready (it should look like dirt and have a pleasant earthy smell), apply it to your garden beds and landscaping as fertilizer. It will nurture your soil and your plants and allow you to water less often. Remember that compost is fertilizer; it should not be used as soil but rather incorporated into your soil a couple of times a year.

Apartment Composting

The common thinking is that not having a yard means you can't compost, but there are some options for all those apartment dwellers out there interested in finding a better home for their scraps than the trash. It just requires a little creative thinking, a small bit of space, and a little commitment (and, to be honest, it's probably not for everyone).

WHAT YOU CAN AND CAN'T COMPOST IN YOUR BACKYARD

CAN BE COMPOSTED

- **Cardboard** (uncoated, small pieces)
- **Coffee grounds and filters**
- **Eggshells**
- **Fireplace ashes** (from natural wood only)
- **Fruits and vegetables**
- **Grass clippings**
- **Hair and fur**
- **Hay and straw**
- **Houseplants**
- **Leaves**
- **Newspaper** (shredded)
- **Nutshells**
- **Paper** (uncoated, small pieces)
- **Sawdust**
- **Tea bags**
- **Wood chips**
- **Yard trimmings**

SHOULD NOT BE COMPOSTED

- **Black walnut tree leaves or twigs** (release substances that might be harmful to plants)
- **Coal or charcoal ash** (might contain substances harmful to plants)
- **Dairy products and eggs*** (create odor problems and attract pests such as rodents and flies)
- **Diseased or insect-ridden plants** (diseases or insects might survive and be transferred to other plants)
- **Fats, grease, lard, oils*** (create odor problems and attract pests such as rodents and flies)
- **Meat or fish bones and scraps*** (create odor problems, attract pests such as rodents and flies, and might also carry pathogens)
- **Pet feces or litter*** (might contain parasites, bacteria, germs, pathogens, and viruses harmful to humans)
- **Yard trimmings treated with chemical pesticides** (might kill beneficial composting organisms)

*These materials should not be composted at home but may be accepted by your community curbside or drop-off composting program. Check with your local composting or recycling coordinator.

Source: U.S. Environmental Protection Agency, "Composting at Home," www2.epa.gov/recycle/composting-home.

The basics of composting discussed previously are not much different when doing it in an apartment—your compost bin still needs air and moisture, a good balance of brown and green (although the ideal balance of these for an indoor system is different from that for a typical outdoor system), and time to do its thing. Because of the time requirement and the likelihood that your bin will be smaller than a typical outdoor bin, it makes sense to have a second bin on standby to swap out when the first gets full (space permitting).

One great option is to set up a worm bin, more technically known as "vermiculture." Worms are surprisingly fast at processing your food scraps, so once you get over any resistance you might have to the concept, you'll likely love this approach. Other options these days are a variety of fancy composting machines that can sit on the counter right next to your toaster oven, as well as "bokashi" systems that actually ferment the waste.

A main difference between apartment and yard composting will be your access to (and proportion of) brown matter, those dead leaves and grasses that make up such an important part of your compost mix. In their place, you can use old newspapers or mail with glossy sections and plastic windows removed. You might also collect fallen leaves from nearby parks or other outdoor spaces if that's an option.

Another important consideration is what you will do with the compost once it's ready. It's perfectly good fertilizer for your houseplants, but they can handle only so much. Most people I've spoken to about apartment composting have stories of supplying many a friend, family member, and neighbor with compost for their houseplants as well. There's even the occasional compost guerrilla who uses his or her compost to fertilize street trees.

Setting Up Indoors. If your apartment has a balcony or rooftop access, set up your compost bin there, in much the same fashion as you would in a backyard. If you're limited to the space inside your apartment, you can still get some compost going with a smaller bin under your sink or in the corner of your kitchen. The easiest thing to do is to buy a commercial kitchen composter that fits your space, but if you're on a budget, a small metal garbage can, a plastic bucket, or even a plastic storage bin will do. Whatever you choose, make sure you have a lid to cover it.

Once you've found the container of your choice, use a drill to make some holes in the top. You need only five or six. This will allow your compost to get the air it needs to properly decompose. You'll also want to put a tray underneath your bin to catch any spills.

Although you're indoors, the process remains pretty similar. Rather than collecting your scraps in a countertop container or a bag in the freezer, throw your food scraps right into the bin as soon as you produce them. Each time you make a deposit, cover your scraps up with some shredded

→ What About Garbage Disposals?

An in-sink garbage disposal is a next-best option for your food scraps after composting. It diverts food from going to landfills, though it typically does not recycle nutrients in the same way as composting. Disposals send food into the sewage system, where it ultimately ends up in your local wastewater treatment facility (unless you have a septic system). Wastewater treatment facilities differ in the way they handle waste. Some create energy with it through a process called *anaerobic digestion*, others send it to be burned or landfilled, and yet others market the sludge as a soil amendment. So the relative value of sending food scraps down a disposal depends first on your ability to compost (commercially or at home) and second on the methods your local water treatment facility uses to treat and dispose of solid wastes. Regardless, using an in-sink disposal to get rid

of food scraps is preferable to sending those scraps directly to the garbage. Even if they ultimately wind up in a landfill, much of the food scraps' decomposition will take place at the wastewater treatment plant, so they won't have the same greenhouse gas implications.

Cooking oils, fats, and greases should *never* be disposed of down the drain, as they can congeal in pipes and potentially contribute to sewage backups. It's also worth checking with your local utility to make sure your pipes and their facility are equipped to handle food waste as part of the sewage system. Finally, be conservative with the amount of water needed to process and flush food in your disposal, so as not to create an additional burden on water usage.

newspaper and a little potting soil. Turn your mixture every two or three days, and keep a close eye on it to see when it's ready to be removed. If you're using two containers, which is recommended, put one aside when it's full and start using the other.

Worm Bins If you really want to supercharge your compost, consider vermiculture. It involves adding special earthworms to your bin that will break down your food scraps a lot faster and produce a much richer compost. It may sound gross, but the results are so effective that you'll soon come to love the little wigglers.

To try this method out, your best bet is to buy a commercially available vermicomposter, as building one yourself can be a bit complicated. From there, you'll want to get your hands on some worms, which you can purchase online or possibly at your local gardening store. Not just any worms will do; red wigglers are typically the best for a worm bin. If you know anyone with a worm bin, just ask for a few of theirs—they multiply very quickly. Load your bin about half full of damp, shredded newspaper scraps (the worms use this as bedding), add some food scraps, and introduce your worms to their new home.

As before, you'll be loading vegetable and fruit food scraps from your kitchen into your bin as you produce them, only this time the scraps will be food for your little tenants. Worms won't eat everything that can go into an outdoor pile, so you'll need to separate out the food scraps they like. Typically, worms prefer fruit and vegetable matter, as well as grains. They will turn their little worm noses up at overly processed or very spicy food, fats and oils, or meat and dairy. If you're freezing your food scraps, you'll need to let them reach room temperature before feeding them to your worms, and be sure the scraps are in smaller pieces so the worms can process them easily. Harvesting compost from a worm bin can be tricky, so research the various possibilities once your bin is ready to see what will work best for you. In short order, you'll have some of the richest compost you can produce, even more nutrient rich than what you might have produced if you had a garden bin.

Other Options If decomposing your food scraps under your sink is not for you, there may still be options. You can try what some hard-core New Yorkers have been known to do and offer your food scraps up at your local

→ Making Energy from Food

A technology that makes energy from food waste is growing rapidly in popularity. Called anaerobic digestion (*anaerobic* means "without oxygen"), the process captures the methane from decomposing food, which can then be used to produce energy. This is much better than allowing the gas to vent uselessly into the atmosphere, as happens in many landfills. (Composting, if aerated properly, does not have the same methane associated with it.) There is still some material left at the end of this process, called digestate, that needs to then be composted in order to be used as a soil amendment. This is an important part of the process for recycling the nutrients back into the cycle, just as is done with regular aerobic composting. Anaerobic digestion is not something you can do at home, but it might be something your city or town or even local grocery store chain is considering doing with its food waste. This trend is a good thing, as anaerobic digestion saves at least one ton of greenhouse gases for every ton of food waste diverted from landfill.[58]

farmers' market. Chances are, one of the vendors at the market will be eager to take them, and you'll be able to bring your scraps in on a weekly basis.

If you don't have any luck there, the Internet is your friend. More and more businesses are popping up to offer local compost collection services, even if it's not done through the regular waste collection in your city. Talk to your building manager about hiring one of these services for your whole building.

Community Composting

Do you reside in a city that offers curbside composting for food waste? If so, consider yourself lucky! San Francisco was the first city to offer this service, but other cities are now joining the ranks. Many cities offer curbside collection for yard trimmings, and more and more communities are considering adding food waste to their curbside collection. In fact, the number of communities in the United States offering curbside composting to their residents grew by 50 percent from 2009 to 2013, at which time it was offered in more than 150 communities in 18 different states.[59]

The beauty of curbside composting is that it is no more difficult or disgusting than taking out the trash. In fact, as one of the lucky ones, I've found it preferable because it makes my garbage bin *less* disgusting. There's no hassle of setting up and maintaining a compost bin; all you have to do is collect your food scraps and give them to someone else to do the dirty work. And as a bonus, most programs allow for meat, bones, and dairy scraps that are not recommended for home composters.

If curbside composting is not yet offered in your community, get busy talking to your local officials and waste-management service people. Let them know you want your community to be responsible with their food scraps.

Go Forth and Go For It

From planning to shopping to storing to cooking to scrapping, you are now armed with all of the information you need to start your journey as a food-waste warrior. Along the way, don't forget that this is a journey. All the waste will not stop immediately. If it happens that some leftovers get moldy, toss them out and try to remind yourself to throw them in the freezer next time. Don't be too hard on yourself.

On the other hand, take stock of where this new mindset comes into play. You might notice that all of a sudden you're taking friends' leftovers home from the restaurant, or packing up extras after the office lunch so that they can be eaten the next day. You might also notice that others find your behavior strange. If so, seize the opportunity to spread the gospel!

Preventing food waste is a perfect challenge for our day because it just screams "crowdsourcing." We need eyes and ears and brains in every nook and cranny if we're really going to turn this thing around. And in my opinion, the only way to do that is through nothing short of a paradigm shift.

That sounds hard, but it's actually very simple. *We just need to value our food.*

Just imagine operating under the belief that food is a really important, valuable asset that takes huge amounts of resources to produce and is in fact critical to our survival. And that because of this belief, it really isn't okay to just waste it.

What would that look like?

When I think about that vision, I see a system that's designed with much more precision as to how much food is needed at every turn and every meal. I see a culture that is more understanding of imperfections and menu items running out, and less tolerant of huge portions that are unlikely to be finished. A mindset where quantity does not equate to value.

But you might see something different. You might see an opportunity to share more of the plums from that prolific tree in your backyard or to invent a new dish using carrot tops and squash peels. You might have an idea for a new way to organize your office parties so that there are not always so many uneaten pastries at the end.

We each encounter waste in different ways, so we each have a different opportunity to prevent it. If we can begin to get our friends, families, readers, and customers to care, it could have a ripple effect to the point of truly streamlining our food system. This new paradigm is the path—a path you have already started on.

PART TWO

RECIPES

It's time to use that use-it-up mindset you've been cultivating. This section contains 20 recipes to help inspire the use of the random assortment of ingredients in your fridge at the end of the week, or of those avocados or bananas that are a bit past their prime.

Some of the recipes, such as Anything Goes Soup and Free-for-All Frittata, are geared toward using up pretty much any vegetable, meat, or grain that needs using. Others are aimed at using up one particular item that often goes bad, such as Buried Avocado Chocolate Mousse and Sour Milk Pancakes (yes, you can bake with milk if it's gone slightly sour!).

The recipes are arranged by meals of the day, with breakfast first and dessert and beverages last. Each lists which items it uses up. But don't stop here. The fun of using things up lies in the wild creativity you can justify unleashing in your kitchen. Dill cream sauce (made from leftover pickle juice) anyone?

Chilaquiles

Makes 4 servings

USES UP

- Stale corn tortillas
- Stale tortilla chips
- Avocado
- Salsa

Just as Parisians dip their stale bread in egg and milk for French toast, cooks in Mexico know to simmer yesterday's tortillas in chili sauce to make a dish called chilaquiles. It is usually served for breakfast or brunch but makes a hearty meal any time of the day, especially topped with onions and cheese. Corn tortillas or tortilla chips are the tortilla of choice, as flour tortillas would get gummy once tossed with the salsa.

12 stale corn tortillas or 6 oz/170 g tortilla chips (about half a large bag)

¼ cup/60 ml vegetable oil, such as sunflower or safflower (if using tortillas)

Salt

1 Tbsp butter

3 cups/720 ml red chili sauce or mild to medium salsa

OPTIONAL GARNISHES

Sliced avocado

Chopped fresh cilantro

Chopped red onion

Grated or crumbled Mexican *cotija*, feta, or Cheddar cheese

If using tortillas, cut them into medium-size wedges. In a large skillet, heat the vegetable oil over medium heat. Working in batches, fry the tortilla wedges until golden brown and crispy, about 1 minute. Transfer to a plate lined with paper towels to drain. Sprinkle with salt.

Drain any remaining oil from the skillet and melt the butter over medium heat. Pour in the chili sauce. Cook until heated through, about 2 minutes.

For crisp chilaquiles: Divide the tortilla wedges or chips among four plates and spoon the sauce over.

For softer chilaquiles: Stir the tortilla wedges or chips into the simmering sauce and cook until softened and heated through, about 1 minute.

Top the chilaquiles with your choice of garnishes, and serve immediately.

Sour Milk Pancakes

Makes about 8 pancakes

USES UP

- Milk that is beginning to sour

Most of us have had the experience of sniffing a carton of milk, making a gruesome face, and going straight to the drain with it. But it turns out there's something better you can do with that milk! Next time you give the sniff test and you're on the fence about it, use it as you would buttermilk in pancakes, waffles, and other baked goods. It's amazing how you won't taste even the slightest bit of bitterness. Of course, you can only eat so many pancakes, so if you know you're not going to get to use milk before it turns sour, put it in the freezer. It may separate a bit when it thaws, but it will be perfectly fine. And if you completely forget about your milk and it's a clotted mess surrounded by a thin, bitter liquid . . . well, it might be time to throw it out.

1 cup/120 g all-purpose flour or whole-wheat flour (or use ½ cup/60 g of each)

2 tsp sugar

¾ tsp salt

½ tsp baking powder

¼ tsp baking soda

1 cup/240 ml sour milk

2 eggs

1 Tbsp neutral-flavored oil, such as light olive, grapeseed, or canola oil

Butter or oil for the pan

OPTIONAL TOPPINGS

Maple syrup

Raspberries, blueberries, sliced strawberries

Sliced banana

Peanut butter or almond butter

In a large bowl, whisk together the flour, sugar, salt, baking powder, and baking soda until well combined. In a medium bowl, beat together the milk, eggs, and oil. Make a well in the center of the dry ingredients and blend in the milk mixture until the batter is smooth.

Heat a large skillet or griddle over medium heat and coat with a little butter.

Ladle ¼ cup/60 ml batter onto the pan to make 4- to 5-in/ 10- to 12-cm pancakes. Cook for 1 to 2 minutes, until bubbles appear and "dry out," then flip and cook for another 1 to 2 minutes on the second side. Repeat with the remaining batter, using more butter for the pan as needed.

Serve warm with the toppings of your choice.

➤ *Planning ahead:* Baked goods freeze very well, so you can bake them up to rescue your sour milk, then freeze them for later. You can even do this with pancakes and waffles: once they're cooled, freeze them solid and store in an airtight container or zip-top bag. Then reheat straight from frozen in a toaster oven or microwave for a real grab-and-go breakfast.

Free-for-All Frittata

Makes 4 to 6 servings

USES UP

- Eggs
- Cheese
- Vegetables

A frittata is basically a big, thick omelet. It's Italian in origin, but there is a similar dish, called a tortilla, that is served in Spain. It is a quick way to work vegetables into breakfast and to work breakfast into every meal of the day. Pack a slice of your frittata with bread for lunch. Serve a wedge for dinner. Leafy greens, squash, tomatoes—they can all be sautéed and added to the skillet right before you pour in the eggs. This is also a good place to use a leftover baked potato if you have one on hand. That hunk of cheese that's been taking up real estate in your refrigerator for months can be used as well; just cut off the mold and shred the rest. You can even add cooked leftovers from earlier meals if you're feeling adventurous, such as stir-fried vegetables or leftover meat. If you are not using any raw vegetables in the frittata, cook the onion 2 to 3 minutes longer, until softened.

8 eggs

Salt and freshly ground black pepper

2 to 3 Tbsp chopped fresh herbs (the smaller amount for the stronger herbs) such as parsley, cilantro, thyme, or tarragon (optional)

1 Tbsp butter, at room temperature

1 Tbsp olive oil, plus more if needed

½ large onion, chopped

3 garlic cloves, minced or pressed (optional)

2 cups/300 g raw, 600 g cooked chopped vegetables: leafy greens, beets, sweet potatoes, green peas, corn kernels, mushrooms, tomatoes, asparagus, or whatever else you have that needs to be used up

1 small boiled or baked potato, diced (optional)

½ cup/60 g shredded semisoft cheese (Cheddar, Gouda, Monterey Jack); ⅓ cup/35 g shredded or grated hard cheese (Parmesan, Asiago, pecorino); or 3 to 5 Tbsp/20 to 40 g crumbled pungent soft cheese (goat cheese, feta, blue cheese)

Preheat the oven to 350°F/180°C.

In a medium bowl, lightly beat the eggs together. Beat in a pinch of salt and pepper and the herbs (if using).

Coat the sides of an oven-safe medium (10-in/25-cm) skillet with the butter. Add the olive oil to the bottom of the pan and heat over medium heat. Add the onion and garlic (if using). Sprinkle with a little salt and cook over medium to medium-low heat until translucent, about 3 minutes.

Add any raw vegetables (except for tender greens) and cook until firm-tender (timing will vary with the vegetable). If the pan seems dry, add a splash more oil. If using tender greens, add them to the pan and cook very briefly, just to wilt. Add any cooked vegetables to the pan, including the potato (if using), season with salt and pepper, and toss to combine everything.

Sprinkle or dot the cheese over the vegetables in the skillet. Pour the eggs evenly over everything. Cook gently on the stovetop over medium heat until the sides are just beginning to set, about 3 minutes.

Transfer to the oven and bake until the top seems to inflate and browns slightly and the eggs are firm and set, 15 to 20 minutes. (Test to see if it's cooked all the way through by pressing the center with your index finger or by inserting an instant-read thermometer into the center—it should register 160°F/71°C.)

Serve warm, cut into wedges.

Anything Goes Soup

Makes 4 to 6 servings

USES UP

- Vegetables
- Cooked grains
- Cooked beans
- Leftover meat
- Fresh herbs
- Various tomato products
- Cheese rinds

Any French chef will tell you that all good soups start with a *mirepoix*—a classic trio of finely chopped onion, carrot, and celery. (And every thrifty French home cook will also tell you that making soup is about using what you have on hand.) The onions are the most important part of the mirepoix trio, and in an absolute pinch you could do without the carrots and celery. As long as your stock is flavorful (be generous with the salt and herbs), you can be as creative as you want with what else you include. Add beans, meat, and/or grains for a bowl that will keep you warm by the fire. Or purée all the ingredients with a bit of cream to impress your guests. Soup usually freezes well, so make a big batch and store some for later. You'll be glad you did.

1 to 2 Tbsp butter or olive oil (or a combination)

1 large onion, finely diced

4 garlic cloves, minced (optional, but very flavorful)

Salt and freshly ground black pepper

2 carrots, finely chopped

2 stalks celery, finely chopped

2 to 3 cups/300 to 450 g cubed, chopped, or shredded raw hard vegetables (such as potatoes, beets, or winter squash), soft vegetables (such as green beans, summer squash, or bell peppers), or greens

8 cups/2 L water or stock

1 cup/200 g chopped fresh or canned tomatoes; or ½ cup/120 ml tomato sauce, tomato purée, pasta sauce, tomato juice, Bloody Mary mix, or taco sauce; or 2 Tbsp tomato paste or ketchup

3 Tbsp chopped fresh herbs (a little less for pungent herbs such as rosemary) or 1 Tbsp dried parsley, dill, basil, or other herbs you have on hand

1 bay leaf (optional)

2 strips fresh or dried lemon zest (optional)

Parmesan rind (optional)

OPTIONAL ADD-INS

1 to 2 cups/65 to 130 g cooked or canned beans, such as chickpeas, kidney beans, pinto beans, cannellini beans, or black beans

8 oz/230 g cut-up cooked chicken, turkey, lean beef or pork, or sausage

1 to 2 cups/250 to 500 g cooked grain, such as rice, quinoa, or barley

In a soup pot, heat the butter over medium heat. Add the onion and garlic (if using), season generously with salt and pepper, and cook, stirring, until the onion begins to soften, about 2 minutes. Add the carrots and celery and cook, stirring, until the carrots begin to soften, about 5 minutes.

If you are using any hard vegetables, add them to the pot with about 1 cup/240 ml of the water, cover, and cook for 5 minutes.

Pour in the remaining 7 cups/1.7 L water and add any soft vegetables. Add the tomatoes, herbs, bay leaf, lemon zest, and Parmesan rind (if using). Season with salt and pepper, more generously if you are using water rather than stock.

Bring to a boil, then turn the heat to low and cook at a simmer, partially covered, for at least 20 minutes, or up to 40 minutes, to develop the flavors and cook the vegetables. If using greens, stir them in now; sturdier greens such as collards and kale will need another 10 minutes of cooking, but soft greens such as chard and spinach can cook just in the residual heat of the soup.

If you are enhancing the soup with any of the add-ins, add them now and simmer for 5 to 10 minutes to heat through and blend the flavors. (Add more water or stock if the soup is not brothy enough for you.) If you used bay leaf, lemon zest, or Parmesan rind, fish them out and discard.

Serve warm. The soup can also be made ahead and almost always tastes better a day or two after it's made.

➤ *Get crazy:* Add leftovers of finished dishes to your soup and see what happens! Spaghetti or fried rice—why not? Add toward the end of the cooking. The effect will, of course, vary depending on what you add.

➤ *Parmesan rind:* If you buy Parmesan cheese by the chunk for grating, save that last impossible-to-grate piece in the freezer. Next time you make soup, toss the rind in. It will add a nice salty richness to the broth.

Gazpacho

Makes 4 to 6 servings

USES UP

- Stale bread
- Damaged/wrinkled tomatoes
- Extra herbs
- Salsa or pasta sauce

This lovely cold soup originated in Andalucía, Spain. There are many versions, but almost all include stale bread. Supermarket sandwich bread will not do very well in this soup. It's best to use sturdier, more rustic bread. But you can cut supermarket bread into cubes and toast it in the oven to make croutons to float on top. Because gazpacho is so flexible, it's a great way to use up extra herbs, such as parsley, cilantro, or basil; extra veggies, such as bell peppers or chile peppers; and, of course, extra tomatoes and tomato products.

1½ cups/75 g cubed stale bread (see headnote)

4 large tomatoes, cut into big chunks (be sure to save all the juices)

1 small or ½ medium cucumber, peeled and cut into big chunks

2 or 3 small garlic cloves, sliced

½ to 1 cup/120 to 240 ml tomato-based salsa or pasta sauce (optional)

Salt

¼ cup/60 ml extra-virgin olive oil

Chopped fresh herbs, such as parsley, cilantro, or basil (optional)

Diced bell pepper (any color) for garnish (optional)

Diced onion for garnish (optional)

Place the bread in a small bowl and cover with cold water. Soak just until softened, 2 to 3 minutes.

Remove the bread and squeeze out the excess water with your hands.

In a blender or food processor, combine the bread, tomatoes, cucumber, and garlic. Purée until smooth. Taste the gazpacho, and add some salsa or pasta sauce, if desired, to amplify the tomato flavor. Season with salt and add the olive oil. Blend again. If using chopped herbs, stir them in now.

Refrigerate for at least 30 minutes, or until well chilled.

Serve garnished with diced bell pepper and onion, if desired.

Sautéed Lettuce

Makes 2 side-dish servings

USES UP

- Lettuce or mixed greens (all kinds)

1 Tbsp butter or olive oil

1 garlic clove, minced

About 5 oz/140 g lettuce or mixed greens, washed, dried, and cut into strips 1 in/2.5 cm wide

⅛ tsp salt

¼ tsp red pepper flakes (optional)

Yes, you absolutely *can* cook lettuce. We cook spinach, kale, cabbage, and other greens; why not lettuce? Both Chinese and French cuisines have a history of cooking lettuce, and it really takes nothing more than a little butter and salt. Try this recipe once and you'll never throw away another half-used bag of mixed greens or partial head of lettuce.

In a large skillet, heat the butter over medium-low heat. Add the garlic and cook, stirring, until tender, about 30 seconds. Add the lettuce, salt, and red pepper flakes (if using) and cook, stirring frequently, until the lettuce is crisp-tender, about 2 minutes.

Serve immediately.

Fried Rice

Makes 4 to 6 servings

USES UP

- Cooked rice
- Raw or cooked meat, poultry, or shrimp
- Raw or cooked vegetables

Forget your measuring cups for this dish. Fried rice is one of those meals where you can throw in a handful of this and a handful of that and everything will turn out more than delicious. It's a great way to use up leftover cooked rice as well as meat or vegetables that have seen fresher days. This recipe works best if you begin with cold rice. Don't try to make it with freshly cooked rice or it will get mushy.

2 eggs

Salt and freshly ground black pepper

3½ Tbsp vegetable oil

1 cup/150 g coarsely chopped raw or cooked vegetables

1 cup/125 g coarsely chopped raw or cooked meat, poultry, shrimp, or firm tofu (optional)

3 or 4 green onions, both white and green parts, thinly sliced

2 garlic cloves, minced

4 cups/1 kg cold cooked rice

1 Tbsp soy sauce

1 tsp agave nectar, maple syrup, or sugar

In a small bowl, beat the eggs and season with salt and pepper.

In a small skillet, heat ½ Tbsp of the vegetable oil over medium-high heat. Add the eggs and cook, stirring constantly, until the eggs are scrambled but still moist, about 30 seconds. Transfer to a plate, set aside to cool slightly, then cut up into smaller pieces.

If using raw vegetables and/or raw meat, in a large skillet, heat 1 Tbsp of the oil. Add the vegetables and/or meat and sauté until both are just cooked through.

Heat the remaining 2 Tbsp oil in the same pan and add the green onions and garlic. Cook, stirring all the while, until they're both tender. Add the rice, soy sauce, agave nectar, cooked eggs, and any already cooked vegetables or meat and cook, stirring constantly, until the rice is piping hot, 4 to 5 minutes.

Serve immediately.

Asian Pasta Salad

Makes 4 servings

USES UP

- Cooked pasta
- Chicken
- Shrimp
- Raw vegetables

If you find yourself with leftover pasta, toss it with a little oil to prevent sticking, and the next day turn it into a tasty salad. (Cooked pasta will keep for at least 3 days in the refrigerator.) Ginger, cilantro, and peanut oil give this salad an Asian kick. But if you don't have these on hand, you can use your favorite dressing to make any number of salads. For example, mix in a little pesto and some cherry tomatoes and cubed mozzarella for an easy Italian-style salad. Is Tex-Mex your thing? Canned black beans, some salsa, corn, and perhaps a little cooked chicken, dressed with lime juice, olive oil, and chili powder will turn last night's pasta into today's Tex-Mex salad. The same tricks also work with leftover rice.

DRESSING

2 Tbsp soy sauce

2 Tbsp lime juice

2 Tbsp peanut oil or dark sesame oil

1½ Tbsp olive oil

1 tsp agave nectar or maple syrup

1 thumb-size knob fresh ginger, peeled and grated

1 garlic clove, crushed through a press

½ tsp red pepper flakes (optional)

Salt (optional)

4 cups/800 g cooked pasta

2 or 3 green onions, both white and green parts, thinly sliced

3 Tbsp chopped fresh basil or mint

3 Tbsp chopped fresh cilantro

1 cup/125 g shredded or diced cooked chicken or shrimp (optional)

1 cup/150 g sliced, shredded, or grated raw vegetables (such as green or red bell peppers, carrot, or cabbage) or shelled and cooked edamame (optional)

Salt (optional)

Chopped roasted peanuts, almonds, or cashews for garnish (optional)

To make the dressing: In a large bowl, whisk together the soy sauce, lime juice, peanut oil, olive oil, agave nectar, ginger, garlic, and red pepper flakes. Season with salt (if needed). Set aside.

Add the pasta, green onions, basil, cilantro, chicken, and vegetables (if using) to the bowl with the dressing and toss to combine. Let sit for 10 to 15 minutes to absorb flavor. This is particularly important if the pasta you're using is a few days old, as it will help soften it as well. Taste the salad and season with salt, if needed (pasta absorbs a lot).

Serve at room temperature, garnished with chopped nuts, if desired.

Broccoli Stalk Salad

Makes 4 to 6 servings

USES UP

- Broccoli stalks
- Avocado
- Carrot

For many of us, the stalks are the lesser half of broccoli. We toss them away in favor of their soft-headed florets. But this salad depends on the stalks for extra crunch, so save them! Broccoli stalks can have a very woody outer layer, especially if the broccoli is large and especially toward the bottom of the stalk. Before you start cutting the stalks into thin ribbons, use a vegetable peeler or paring knife to remove the tough skin. Adding carrot and avocado makes the dish creamy and sweet—and a delicious departure from the usual bowl of boiled vegetables. You can also chop the broccoli and carrot for more of a slaw effect; dice the avocado and add it just before serving.

DRESSING

¼ cup/60 ml extra-virgin olive oil

3 Tbsp red wine vinegar, white wine vinegar, or cider vinegar

2 tsp honey

¼ tsp kosher salt

Freshly ground black pepper

4 large broccoli stalks (not the florets!), shaved with a vegetable peeler or very thinly sliced (see headnote)

1 carrot, shaved into long, thin strips with a vegetable peeler

¼ to ½ cup/25 to 50 g thinly sliced red onion

½ to 1 avocado, cut into ⅛-in/4-mm slices

Small fresh basil, cilantro, or parsley leaves for garnish (optional)

To make the dressing: In a small bowl, whisk together the olive oil, vinegar, honey, and salt. Season with pepper. Measure out 2 Tbsp of dressing and set aside.

In a medium bowl, combine the broccoli, carrot, onion, and remaining dressing. Let sit for 30 minutes at room temperature to allow the broccoli to soften. (Taste and adjust the seasoning with a little more vinegar, salt, and pepper, if desired.)

Mound the salad on plates, top with the avocado, and drizzle with the reserved 2 Tbsp dressing. Garnish with fresh herb leaves, if desired, before serving.

Light Chicken Salad

Makes 3 or 4 servings

USES UP

- Cooked chicken
- Herbs
- Fruit
- Vegetables

Chicken salad doesn't have to drown in mayo. This recipe is a great way to turn last night's extra chicken into a light Mediterranean salad. The red wine vinegar and honey give the dressing a sweet-tart kick, but for an even simpler version, you could make a beautiful meal with just the chicken, salt, olive oil, and herbs. To make the salad a bit more substantial, mix in some chopped seeds or nuts, cut-up fresh or dried fruit, cut-up raw vegetables, or chopped cooked root vegetables. This salad is great served on a sandwich or over a bed of greens with a hunk of fresh bread.

¼ cup/60 ml extra-virgin olive oil

¼ cup/60 ml red wine vinegar

1 Tbsp honey

Salt and freshly ground black pepper

2 cups/250 g shredded or diced cooked chicken (breast or thigh or a combination)

2 green onions, both white and green parts, chopped

¼ to ⅓ cup/7 to 20 g chopped fresh herbs (parsley, mint, tarragon, cilantro, or a combination)

ADD-INS

Nuts: almonds, walnuts, pistachios

Seeds: sunflower, pumpkin

Fresh fruit: finely chopped apples, nectarines, pineapple, pomegranate seeds,

Dried fruit: finely chopped apricots, pears, cranberries

Raw vegetables: finely chopped celery, carrot, cabbage, bell pepper, grape tomatoes

Cooked vegetables: finely chopped sweet potatoes, parsnips, rutabaga, beets, butternut squash

Bread and/or greens for serving

In a small bowl, whisk together the olive oil, vinegar, and honey. Season with salt and pepper.

In a large bowl, combine the chicken, green onions, and herbs. Mix in your choice of add-ins, add the dressing, and toss to coat.

Serve as a sandwich filling or mounded on a bed of greens.

After-Party Crusted Chicken

Makes 6 servings

USES UP

- Potato or tortilla chips, crackers, croutons, and/or appetizer toasts

2 lb/910 g boneless, skinless chicken breasts or thighs, cut into strips ½ in/12 mm wide

Salt and freshly ground black pepper

1 cup/120 g all-purpose flour

2 tsp seasoning, such as onion powder, paprika, or your favorite spice rub (optional)

2 eggs

1 cup/240 ml milk

1½ cups/340 g tortilla or potato chip and/or cracker crumbs

In some families, beautifully fried chicken is the stuff of tradition, with top-secret recipes passed down from one generation to the next. This baked version is a foolproof way to achieve a crisp crust and use up all the chips left after your last party. You'll need in the neighborhood of 12 oz/340 g of tortilla chips, potato chips, *thin* crackers, croutons, or *thin* appetizer toasts to get the necessary amount of crumbs. Break them into smallish pieces and pulse-grind them in a food processor until they are the texture of coarse coffee grounds. You can also use the crumb coating on fish or tofu. Bake fish for 8 to 10 minutes, depending on the thickness. Tofu will take about 10 minutes, long enough to set the coating and heat the tofu through.

Preheat the oven to 400°F/200°C. Line a rimmed baking sheet with parchment paper.

With a paper towel, pat the chicken pieces dry. Season with salt and pepper.

In a wide, shallow bowl, combine the flour and seasoning (if using). In a second wide, shallow bowl, whisk together the eggs and milk. Place the crumbs in a third wide, shallow bowl.

Arrange the chicken, flour mixture, egg mixture, and crumbs next to the prepared baking sheet, in that order.

Dredge the chicken in the flour mixture, then in the eggs and milk, allowing the excess to drip off, and finally in the crumbs, pressing to adhere. Place on the baking sheet in a single layer.

Bake until the crust is lightly colored (it will remain pale; don't wait for golden brown) and the chicken is cooked through, about 20 minutes. Cooking times will vary; chicken thighs may take about 5 minutes longer than breasts.

Serve immediately.

Shepherd's Pie

Makes 6 servings

USES UP

- Cooked meat
- Potatoes
- Herbs

This iconic British dish not only defines comfort food, it also gives you a way to stretch last night's roast or ground meat into a second meal. Lamb is traditional in shepherd's pie, but any meat works for this. The classic topping is mashed potatoes, but you can also cap the pie with a layer of sliced cooked potatoes—either boiled or baked. If the leftover meat is from a roast of some type, include the pan juices or gravy along with the stock or water.

2 Tbsp butter, plus more for dotting the top

1 onion, chopped

2 Tbsp flour

1½ cups/360 ml stock or water

2 tsp fresh thyme leaves or 1 tsp dried thyme

1 to 2 Tbsp chopped fresh leafy herbs, such as parsley, dill, basil, or cilantro, plus more for garnish

Salt and freshly ground black pepper

2 cups/250 g cooked ground meat or minced roasted meat, such as beef, pork, lamb, chicken, or turkey

1 lb/455 g potatoes, cooked and mashed or sliced

Preheat the oven to 375°F/190°C.

In a large saucepan, melt the butter over medium-low heat. Add the onion and cook until just beginning to soften, about 1 minute. Sprinkle with the flour and cook, stirring constantly, until the mixture turns light golden, about 2 minutes. Pour in the stock and bring to a boil. Add the thyme and leafy herbs and season with salt and pepper (be cautious if the meat you are using was already heavily seasoned). Lower the heat to a simmer and cook for 4 minutes. Add the meat to the pan and cook for 1 minute, until heated through.

Scrape the mixture into a 9-in/23-cm pie plate or an 8-by-8-in/20-by-20-cm baking dish. Spoon the potatoes on top to cover. If using sliced potatoes, lay them on top of the meat so that the slices overlap slightly. Dot the pie with a few pieces of butter (use more for plain sliced potatoes) and sprinkle with salt.

Bake until the pie has a golden crust, about 45 minutes.

Let sit for 10 minutes before serving.

Tacos Your Way

Makes 8 tacos

USES UP

· Cooked meat
· Vegetables
· Cheese
· Tortillas

There's something about folding your meal into a warm envelope of corn that gives tired ingredients new *vida*. Tacos are a great way to use up leftover meat and veggies that are approaching their final days, simply by sautéing them and topping with a delicious taco sauce. But if you're not in the mood for Mexican, don't let that stop you. Almost anything can go into a tortilla and taste better for it. There are no rules in taco land. Make it an Indian taco by using curry spice and chutney instead of taco sauce. For a taste of the Southern United States, use barbecue sauce and collard greens. Make a zingy cabbage slaw with an apple cider dressing, pile heaps of it into a tortilla, and top with toasted sunflower seeds. There are no limits to what can go in a taco. Here, however, I start you off with the classic approach.

TACO SAUCE

2 tsp oil, such as olive oil, sunflower oil, or peanut oil

½ onion, finely chopped

2 garlic cloves, finely chopped

1 tsp ground cumin

Pinch of cayenne or other chili powder (optional)

Salt

8 oz/225 g canned tomato sauce

1 tsp dried oregano

8 corn tortillas

1 Tbsp sunflower or other vegetable oil, plus 2 tsp

2 cups/300 g sliced or diced raw vegetables, such as bell peppers, summer squash, winter squash, carrots, cabbage, broccoli stalks

Salt and freshly ground black pepper

1 tsp ground cumin

1 cup/125 g minced, pulled, or ground cooked meat, such as beef, pork, lamb, chicken, or turkey, or coarsely chopped firm tofu

1 tsp dried oregano

OPTIONAL TOPPINGS

Diced avocado

Chopped fresh cilantro

Chopped lettuce

Grated or shredded cheese

Lime wedges for squeezing

To make the taco sauce: In a small saucepan, heat the oil over medium heat. Add the onion, garlic, cumin, cayenne (if using), and a pinch of salt and cook until the onion is translucent, 2 to 3 minutes. (Add a splash of water if the pan looks dry.) Add the tomato sauce and oregano, turn the heat to medium-low, and cook for 5 minutes, stirring occasionally, to blend the flavors. The sauce should be the consistency of pasta sauce; add a splash of water if it starts to get too thick.

Heat a large cast-iron skillet over high heat. Working in batches, add the tortillas with as little overlap as possible, and heat until they begin to puff just slightly. Wrap in a kitchen towel to keep them warm.

In the same skillet, heat the 1 Tbsp sunflower oil over medium-high heat Add the vegetables, season with salt and pepper, and cook until softened (the timing will depend on the vegetable and how finely it's been cut). Remove from the pan and set aside.

In the same pan, heat the remaining 2 tsp oil over medium heat. Add the cumin and stir until the oil is fragrant, about 30 seconds. Add the meat and oregano, stirring to coat with the oil. Add half of the taco sauce, toss to combine with the meat, and cook until heated through, 1 to 2 minutes.

Sprinkle each tortilla with a bit of salt, then fill first with meat, then vegetables. Top with some of the remaining taco sauce and your choice of toppings. Serve immediately.

➡ *What to do with stale tortillas:* Tear older tortillas into medium pieces and add to a bowl of soup or beans, instead of adding rice or pasta. Or make homemade tortilla chips by cutting the tortillas into 1½-in/4-cm wedges and frying them in a hot skillet with oil or butter until crispy and golden brown. Set on a plate lined with paper towels to soak up any excess oil. Sprinkle with salt and enjoy. Also, see the recipe for Chilaquiles (page 120).

Drunken Marinated Meat

Makes 6 to 8 servings

USES UP

- Red wine
- Fresh herbs

1 to 1½ cups/240 to 360 ml red wine

½ cup/120 ml olive oil

⅓ cup/80 ml soy sauce

¼ cup/85 g honey (optional)

½ cup/75 g chopped onion

5 garlic cloves, minced

1½ tsp salt

A few grinds of black pepper

Sprigs of fresh rosemary or parsley (optional)

1½ to 2 lb/680 to 910 g meat, poultry, fish, tempeh, or tofu

A bottle of wine that's been open for a few days doesn't make for fine drinking, but it's perfect for cooking. No need to buy a new bottle for a recipe when you already have one that's half full. The alcohol in this marinade deepens flavors, and it nicely flavors other proteins, such as poultry, thick fish steaks, tempeh, and tofu. You can also use it for soft vegetables such as zucchini, eggplant, mushrooms, and summer squash. The marinating time will be considerably shorter, 30 minutes to 2 hours. Lighter-colored foods will take on some color from the red wine–soy mixture. Choose a container that will allow the protein you are marinating to be submerged (deep if you're doing a roast, for example, or shallow if you're marinating cubes).

In the marinating container, whisk together the wine, olive oil, soy sauce, honey (if using), onion, garlic, salt, and a few grinds of pepper. Add fresh herb sprigs, if desired.

Add the meat, cover, and refrigerate for at least 4 hours, or up to 1 day. If the protein isn't submerged in the marinade, turn it over once or twice so that all sides have spent some time in the marinade.

You can then bake, broil, grill, or pan-fry the marinated food. Consult a good basic cookbook for timing, based on the type of protein, the cut, and your chosen method of preparation. If you have marinated raw meat, poultry, or seafood, discard the marinade; or if you choose to use it as a sauce, transfer to a saucepan, bring to a boil, and simmer for at least 3 minutes before serving.

Banana Sorbet

Makes 2 servings

USES UP

· Overripe bananas

2 overripe bananas

2 Tbsp lime juice

1½ tsp maple syrup or agave nectar (optional)

This "sorbet" is easy, cheap, healthful, and delicious. What could be better? It takes no time at all and is a great way to use up overripe bananas. Anytime you have a banana that is past its prime, just peel, slice, and freeze. Having frozen peeled bananas on hand means you can whip up a super-quick dessert whenever you're in the mood. If your bananas are very sweet, you might choose to omit the sweetener, but I particularly like the flavor of maple syrup with bananas.

Peel the bananas, cut into ½-in/12-mm chunks, and freeze until hardened, about 2 hours.

In a food processor, combine the banana chunks, lime juice, and maple syrup (if using) and pulse until smooth or slightly chunky, as desired.

The "sorbet" is best served right away, but you can freeze it in an airtight container, though the texture will change slightly.

Buried Avocado Chocolate Mousse

Makes 4 servings

USES UP

- Overripe avocados
- Fruit
- Nuts

This brilliant dessert substitutes all the smooth creaminess of an avocado for the less healthful ingredients that are typically in chocolate mousse. And you won't even notice. It's delightfully smooth, and the chocolate easily covers up the flavor of a slightly overripe avocado. Go wild with the toppings and you'll have a sundae even your gym trainer would be proud of. If you don't have any milk on hand, don't worry; the mousse will be just fine without it. But if you do you have some available, add it for a looser, smoother mousse.

2 large ripe or slightly overripe avocados (see Note)

¼ cup/60 ml milk, milk substitute, or yogurt (optional)

½ cup/60 ml agave nectar, maple syrup, honey, or superfine sugar, plus more if desired

5 Tbsp unsweetened cocoa powder, plus more if desired

1½ tsp vanilla extract

⅛ tsp salt

OPTIONAL TOPPINGS

Raspberries, blueberries, sliced strawberries

Sliced banana

Shredded coconut, toasted

Candied citrus peel

Chopped nuts

Whipped cream (the mousse is so healthful, you can splurge here if you want)

Scoop the avocado flesh into a food processor. Add the milk (if using), agave nectar, cocoa powder, vanilla, and salt and process until free of lumps and velvety in texture. Taste and add more sweetener if it's not sweet enough for you; or add more cocoa powder (just 1 tsp at a time) if you want a darker chocolate flavor. (Alternatively, if making by hand, mash the avocados with a fork first, then mash in the remaining ingredients.)

Serve plain or with one of the toppings. The mousse will keep for at least 1 week in an airtight container in the refrigerator, but honestly it's so delicious that the chances of it lasting that long are slim.

➡ *Note:* If you have small avocados, blend them with 5 Tbsp sweetener, 3 Tbsp cocoa, 1 tsp vanilla, and a small pinch of salt. Taste, then add small amounts of cocoa and/or sweetener until you hit a balance of sweet to chocolate that you like.

Sneaky Black Bean Brownies

Makes 16 brownies

USES UP

· Black beans

My husband is part Cuban and grew up with beans as a regular part of his week. These days, my mother-in-law, Judy, throws a few extra dried beans in the pot and then makes these amazing brownies alongside her beans and rice. Cooking your own beans can save money and packaging, but it's easy to accidentally make enough for a small army. When you've had your fill of burritos, these brownies are a clever way to sneak leftover beans into a favorite sweet. The beans up the protein in each brownie, but their flavor is so subtle you'll never know they're there. The brownies also happen to be delicious, super fudgy, and gluten-free. If you've got mini chocolate chips, use them here; they'll break down a little more easily in the food processor.

2 cups/430 g cooked black beans

½ cup/40 g quick-cooking oats (see Note)

2 Tbsp unsweetened cocoa powder

2 Tbsp light brown sugar

⅓ cup/80 ml agave nectar or maple syrup

¼ cup/60 ml coconut oil, light olive oil, vegetable oil, or melted butter

2 tsp vanilla extract

½ tsp baking powder

¼ tsp salt

⅔ cup/100 g dark or semi-sweet chocolate chips

½ cup/40 g shredded coconut (optional)

Preheat the oven to 350°F/180°C. Grease an 8-by-8-in/20-by-20-cm baking pan.

In a food processor, combine the beans, oats, cocoa powder, brown sugar, agave nectar, coconut oil, vanilla, baking powder, salt, and chocolate chips and process until almost smooth (you'll still have small pieces of chocolate chips in the batter). Stir in the coconut (if using). Scrape the mixture into the prepared baking pan. Bake for 30 to 35 minutes, or until a wooden pick inserted in the center comes out with some moist crumbs attached.

Cool completely before cutting into 16 squares. If you've got the time, chill them in the refrigerator before cutting and serving.

➤ *Note:* Quick-cooking oats are simply rolled oats that have been ground up into smaller pieces to make them cook more quickly. If you have only regular rolled oats (sometimes called old-fashioned oats), just pulse-grind them in the food processor before adding the other ingredients.

Herbed Butter

Makes about ¼ cup/60 g

USES UP

· Fresh herbs

So often we buy herbs for a recipe that calls for only 2 to 3 Tbsp and then watch the rest of the bunch go to mush. This is a chef's trick for transforming that surplus cilantro, rosemary, thyme, or tarragon into a gourmet condiment. You can spread herbed butter on bread, fold a spoonful into a bowl of pasta, or melt a dollop on top of grilled meat. It's impossible to go wrong with this one. If you have a lot of herbs, double or triple the recipe and scrape the herb butter into an ice-cube tray. When frozen, pop the cubes out of the tray and transfer to a zip-top freezer bag to store. Label the bag so you remember what herbs you used.

4 Tbsp/55 g butter, at room temperature

2 to 3 Tbsp finely chopped fresh herbs (use the smaller amount for pungent herbs such as rosemary or oregano and the larger amount for soft, leafy herbs such as basil or dill)

Salt (optional)

In a small bowl, combine the butter and herbs. If using unsalted butter, season with a little salt (if desired). Mash until evenly blended.

If not serving immediately, store in the refrigerator, tightly wrapped, for up to 6 days, or freeze for up to 2 months.

Quick and Easy Refrigerator Pickles

Makes one 1-qt/1-L jar of pickles

USES UP

· Wrinkly vegetables (or fruits if you're feeling adventurous)

Gone are the days when pickles were made only from cucumbers and used primarily on sandwiches. Now chefs are pickling just about everything: carrots, pattypan squash, cherry tomatoes, okra, even stone fruit. But they aren't just a kick to the taste buds. The brine locks in flavor and crispness better than the crisper drawer ever could, it also keeps produce from spoiling. This technique is also great for garden surplus that never ripens, such as green tomatoes. If you're mixing and matching vegetables, it's best to pickle vegetables of like density—for example, carrots and turnips, cucumbers and green tomatoes.

Vegetables to loosely fill a 1-qt/1-L canning jar

BRINE

1½ cups/360 ml distilled white or cider vinegar

1 cup/240 ml water

¼ cup/50 g sugar or 2 Tbsp sugar plus 2 Tbsp honey (optional, if you like sweet pickles)

2 Tbsp coarse salt

1 bay leaf

1 Tbsp brown or yellow mustard seeds

1 tsp whole black peppercorns

1 tsp fennel seeds (optional)

½ tsp red pepper flakes (optional)

Pack the vegetables into a sterilized 1-qt/1-L canning jar, leaving about 1 in/2.5 cm of room at the top.

To make the brine: In a medium saucepan, combine the vinegar, water, sugar, salt, bay leaf, mustard seeds, peppercorns, and fennel seeds and red pepper flakes (if using). Cook over medium heat, stirring, until the sugar and salt have dissolved. Bring to a boil.

Pour the brine into the jar to completely cover the vegetables. Cool to room temperature, and seal with the lid once cooled. After it's sealed, tip the jar upside down to evenly distribute the spices. Refrigerate for at least 1 day to let the flavors develop, or for up to 1 month.

Infused Vodka

Makes 3 cups/720 ml

USES UP

- Softening fruits
- Citrus peels
- Fresh herbs
- Ginger
- Cucumbers
- Chile peppers

On the road to less food waste, there is definitely time for a cocktail. This list of ingredients you can use to infuse vodka with flavor is just a start. Intrepid infusion makers have experimented with everything from orange rinds to bacon. Be creative and, if you like, try pairing a couple of ingredients together. For example, coconut, pineapple, and ginger would make a nice tropical vodka; cucumber and mint would be a refreshing combo; and a mix of berries with just one or two chile peppers would be fruity and spicy. If you've got a vanilla bean that you've used once, rinse and dry it and add it to one of your infusions for a mild vanilla note.

INFUSION INGREDIENTS

Sliced almonds, toasted

Pecans, toasted and chopped

Shredded coconut, toasted

Cucumbers, peeled and sliced

Fresh mint or basil, bruised

Ginger, sliced

Citrus with peel, such as lemons, oranges, tangerines, limes, or ruby grapefruit, cut into 1-in/2.5-cm chunks

Stone fruit, such as peaches, nectarines, apricots, or plums, quartered and pitted

Cherries, sweet or tart, whole or pitted

Apples, peeled, quartered, and cored

Pears, peeled, quartered, and cored

Berries

Pineapple, peeled and finely chopped

Fresh chile peppers (use only 1 or 2 chiles)

3 cups/720 ml vodka

Sparkling water for serving (optional)

If you're using fresh fruits, herbs, or vegetables as infusion ingredients, wash them well. Place the infusion ingredients in a 1-qt-/1-L glass jar with a lid.

Pour the vodka over the infusion ingredients, seal, and place in a cool, dark spot. Taste after 3 days to see if it's at the level you'd like. Potent ingredients such as ginger or chile peppers will infuse the vodka faster than milder ones such as almonds or coconut. (If you're using an extremely hot chile, taste after 24 hours!)

Taste again on the fourth day and continue tasting until the vodka is as flavorful as you desire, up to 1 month. Strain and discard the infusion ingredients. Note that certain soft fruit such as apples and pears will make the vodka cloudy, but it's fine to drink.

Enjoy your new beverage with some sparkling water to fully experience the infused flavor, or use in your cocktail of choice. Store in the freezer; the infusion will keep for several months.

PART THREE

DIRECTORY

Did you know that fresh basil is best stored like fresh-cut flowers? That's right: Basil lasts longer when stored at room temperature with its stems in a glass of water, rather than in the refrigerator. Asparagus does well in standing water, too, but in the refrigerator. Artichokes should go in the refrigerator, but it's best to sprinkle them with water after chopping off the ends. Knowing how to store your fruits and vegetables properly will extend their life, buying you time to make sure you can use them up. The same goes for other foods as well.

This Directory refers to a few types of containers. While plastic bags and paper towels can work, in the spirit of being waste free, I encourage you to invest in reusable containers and bags.

Breathable bag:

This is typically a perforated plastic bag but could also be a reusable cloth bag that is left open. A mesh bag is too breathable. A container with holes, such as the type that berries come in, could work as well.

Airtight container:

This could be a closed glass, plastic, or stainless-steel food storage container, or a zip-top bag.

Cloth:

A cloth napkin works well, but you could also use a paper towel.

Make sure to thoroughly wash containers between uses

This Directory provides specific information about many of the foods in your kitchen. As you'll see, it offers advice on how to store foods, how to freeze them, and how long they stay at their best quality. It also has helpful tidbits on ways to use parts that you might have thought were inedible, tips for reviving foods, and answers to questions like, "What are those brown spots?"

There are a few important points to keep in mind when using this section. First, **the time frames given for when products are "At Freshest" are estimates of just that: How**

long a given food will be at its best. It does not mean the product is unsafe or needs to be thrown out after that time is up, but rather that you should aim to use it within that time frame to have the best experience. Unless otherwise noted, I encourage you to still taste, smell, and try to use the product after that time period. It might be better to cook the food than to eat it raw or by itself. Alternatively, if you don't think you'll use the product within that time frame, it's probably a good idea to freeze it.

Second, **the best way to store food depends on how quickly you will use it.** Some of the suggestions in this Directory might surprise you. For instance, you might be accustomed to keeping nuts in the pantry, but unless you're going to use them within a week or two, optimal storage is in the refrigerator. This is true for many products, including produce. They can stay at room temperature for a period of time, but will last much longer when kept in the refrigerator.

Ultimately, buying less food more frequently is the key to fresh, nutritious food. Long-term storage for most products is less desirable. Nevertheless, many of us do buy in large quantities, and this Directory

will arm you with the information you need to preserve those products for as long as possible.

Finally, **use your judgment.** Knowing how long a food will last is not a perfect science. Information for this Directory came from the best sources I could find—government agencies, books on the science and preservation of food, trade associations that represent the specific products, and product manufacturers themselves.[60] However, only you know if the product sat in a hot car for too long or was left on the counter. Only you can smell it. And only you know if you'll actually remember to take it out of the freezer and use it. So use this Directory as a guide, but use your judgment as well.

Fruits

APPLES

REFRIGERATOR: Yes

AT FRESHEST: Up to 6 weeks in the refrigerator, longer in a root cellar environment

OPTIMAL STORAGE: Do not wash until ready to use. Store in a breathable bag in the low-humidity drawer of the refrigerator. Handle carefully to prevent bruising, and separate any with bruises from other apples (or they will cause others to brown). Apples ripen 6 to 10 times faster at room temperature.

For large quantities, store in a cardboard box covered with a damp towel in a root cellar or other cool place. Ideally, you would wrap each apple individually in newspaper to reduce their influence on each other. Many heirloom varieties are not suited for long-term storage, so try to eat them right away.

FREEZING: Can be frozen raw or cooked, with or without sugar.

Raw—Wash, peel (if desired), core, and slice. To prevent browning, either blanch for 1½ to 2 minutes or sprinkle with lemon juice. Then choose between (1) packing dry with ½ cup/100 g sugar per 1 qt/1 kg of apples; (2) packing in 40 percent syrup (see page 155); or (3) placing directly on a baking sheet and freezing, then transferring to an airtight container.

Cooked—Cook, cool, and pack in an airtight container.

USE IT UP/REVIVAL: To prevent apple slices from browning, toss them with one part citrus juice and three parts water.

Mealy or wrinkled—Cook! Even shriveled apples can be cooked into applesauce, apple pies, apple crisps, etc. A few bruises are fine and can be cut out; if the whole fruit is soft or mushy, however, discard.

Use apple peels to make a tea, flavor fresh water, make a jelly or syrup, or in smoothies.

AVOCADOS

REFRIGERATOR: After ripe

AT FRESHEST: Whole, after ripe, 2 to 5 days in refrigerator

OPTIMAL STORAGE: Store on the counter until ripe, then refrigerate loose. Place in a closed paper bag to accelerate ripening (adding an apple or banana will make them ripen even faster). Do not refrigerate before ripe, or they will never ripen.

Store avocado-based products such as guacamole with plastic wrap pressed directly onto the surface of the food to avoid browning.

✳ **FREEZING:** Peel, purée, mix in 1 Tbsp lemon juice per avocado, and pack into an airtight container, leaving ½ in/12 mm at the top for expansion.

↻ **USE IT UP/REVIVAL:** If you find that an avocado is not ripe enough after you've cut it open, sprinkle the surface with lemon or lime juice, close it back up around the pit, wrap tightly, and place in the refrigerator. Check periodically to see if it has ripened enough to eat.

To prevent browning once cut, close the avocado back up around the pit or sprinkle with lemon or lime juice and place in an airtight container in the refrigerator.

If your avocado or guacamole has turned brown, skim off the brown (oxidized) parts. Parts that are green are still edible (so are the brown parts, but they may not taste as good).

BANANAS

▥ **REFRIGERATOR:** Optional after ripe

◉ **AT FRESHEST:** Less ripe, 5 to 7 days; ripe, 1 to 2 days

◔ **OPTIMAL STORAGE:** Remove any plastic wrapping. Store on the counter at room temperature, away from other fruit (unless you're trying to ripen those fruit). Once ripe, you can store them in the refrigerator. The skin may darken, but the banana will be just right for several days.

✳ **FREEZING:** Bananas can be frozen with or without the peel, but the peel can be difficult to remove when frozen. It's best to peel them and store in an airtight container. If leaving the peel on, place loose in the freezer and, when ready to use, cut off both ends and slide a knife under the peel to loosen.

↻ **USE IT UP/REVIVAL:** Browning or spotted bananas are perfectly fine to eat.

Bruised parts of bananas may be easily cut away or used.

Very brown or nearly black bananas and frozen bananas are great for baking quick breads, muffins, or cakes.

BERRIES (strawberries, raspberries, blueberries, blackberries)

▥ **REFRIGERATOR:** Yes

◉ **AT FRESHEST:** Raspberries, blackberries, and strawberries, 2 to 3 days; blueberries, 10 days

◔ **OPTIMAL STORAGE:** Do not wash until ready to use.

Blueberries—Store either in their original container or in a covered bowl or container.

Raspberries, blackberries, and strawberries—Store on a shelf in the refrigerator in a single layer in an aerated container on a tray lined with cloth, and then cover loosely with another cloth. If space is constrained, add second and third layers with cloths between them. For strawberries, leave the green caps on until ready to eat. (The green caps are edible, but not that tasty. It's no problem to leave them on when making smoothies.)

✳ **FREEZING: Blueberries**—Rinse, dry, and pack loosely into rigid airtight containers.

Raspberries and blackberries—Rinse, dry, place separated on a baking sheet, and freeze, then transfer to airtight containers.

Strawberries—Rinse, dry, remove stems, place uncovered with cut side down on a baking sheet lined with wax paper, and freeze, then transfer to an airtight container.

Many recipes don't require thawing the berries; if a recipe does require thawing the berries, let them sit at room temperature for an hour or so. If necessary, transfer to a colander to drain. You can capture the juice and use it to flavor drinks or for other recipes.

↻ **USE IT UP/REVIVAL:** If a small amount of berries in a container show mold, do not discard the entire container. Pick through the container and throw away those that are obviously bad. Do this as soon as possible to prevent mold from spreading.

To bring out the flavor of lackluster berries, put them in a bowl (hull and slice strawberries first), sprinkle with a little sugar, and let sit for 15 minutes. The sugar will draw the moisture from the berries to make a sweet natural syrup.

CITRUS

🗄 **REFRIGERATOR:** Yes

◉ **AT FRESHEST:** Counter, 4 to 5 days; refrigerator, 3 to 8 weeks

⬛ **OPTIMAL STORAGE:** Store loose in the low-humidity crisper drawer. Do not put in a plastic bag or airtight container. Peeled or cut oranges should be refrigerated in an airtight container or bag. If you have a citrus tree, the best way to store is to leave the fruit on the tree until you are ready to use. Citrus can stay good for months on the tree.

✳ **FREEZING:** Rinse, peel, divide into sections, and remove seeds and membranes. Slice if desired. Then pack in 40 percent syrup (see page 155). Citrus can be frozen in water or juice without the sugar, but may have a less desirable texture and color and will take longer to thaw. Navel oranges can become quite bitter when frozen.

↻ **USE IT UP/REVIVAL:** Citrus can be ripe even if the rind is still green in places.

The inside of citrus may be good even if the peel shows signs of damage. Open and investigate before tossing.

Fruit that has slight discoloration, normally a small amount of brown around the seeds, is usually acceptable to eat.

Peels/rinds—Often called "zest," the outer portion of citrus peels can be used to flavor soups, stews, or pasta sauces. Use a vegetable peeler to pull strips of zest (the thin, colored outer portion of the peel) off the fruit, arrange on a plate, and let dry (in nonhumid weather, this should take 1 to 2 days). Then store in a jar in the pantry. The strips can also be candied and, in China's Sichuan province, are pickled.

Citrus peels have numerous uses around the house, such as to make cleaning supplies.

FIGS

▥ **REFRIGERATOR:** Yes

◉ **AT FRESHEST:** 2 to 3 days

◷ **OPTIMAL STORAGE:** Do not wash until ready to use. Arrange in a single layer in a cloth-lined, aerated or uncovered container.

✳ **FREEZING:** Wash and place separated on a baking sheet and freeze, then transfer to an airtight container.

↻ **USE IT UP/REVIVAL:** Figs that have gotten too soft for your liking (but are not showing signs of decay) can be stewed or boiled and made into sauces and marinades.

GRAPES

▥ **REFRIGERATOR:** Yes

◉ **AT FRESHEST:** 2 weeks

◷ **OPTIMAL STORAGE:** Do not wash until ready to use. Keep unwashed bunches (grapes still on their stems) in a paper or breathable bag on a shelf in the refrigerator.

✳ **FREEZING:** Wash, dry, place separated on a baking sheet and freeze, then transfer into an airtight container. A single grape cluster can also be frozen whole.

↻ **USE IT UP/REVIVAL:** If a small amount of grapes in a container show mold or are wrinkled, do not discard the entire container. Pick through and throw away those that are obviously bad. Do this as soon as possible to prevent mold from spreading.

The powdery white coating on grapes is called bloom and is a naturally occurring substance that protects grapes from moisture loss and decay.

Frozen grapes are their own mini-sorbet bites. This is a fantastic thing to do with grapes that you might not get around to eating in time.

MELONS

▥ **REFRIGERATOR:** After ripe

◉ **AT FRESHEST:** Whole, 5 to 15 days, depending on ripeness; cut, 3 to 5 days in refrigerator

◷ **OPTIMAL STORAGE:** If unripe, store whole in a cool, dry place out of sunlight. Once ripe, store on a shelf in the refrigerator. Refrigerate cut melon, regardless of ripeness, wrapped or in airtight container. If possible, do not remove the seeds from the remaining sections of cut melon, as they keep the flesh from drying out. For watermelons, avoid storing them near apples, bananas, peaches, and avocados unless trying to ripen quickly.

✳ **FREEZING:** Remove the rind and cube the flesh. Place separate on a baking sheet and freeze, then transfer to an airtight container. Frozen melons are best used straight from the freezer in smoothies, margaritas, or other blended drinks.

↻ **USE IT UP/REVIVAL:** Melons often have discoloration or deformed husks/rinds. This is no reason to discard them—check the inside before throwing a melon away. Melons that have spoiled often have an unpleasant odor and are overly soft.

The white part of watermelon rind can be pickled—an old favorite in the Southern United States.

Watermelon seeds, even the black ones, are edible and can be toasted as you would pumpkin seeds for a nutritious snack.

Melons should be washed before eating, even though the rind is not eaten.

PEARS

▤ **REFRIGERATOR:** After ripe

◔ **AT FRESHEST:** After ripe, 5 days in refrigerator

⬒ **OPTIMAL STORAGE:** Do not wash until ready to use. Leave firm, unripe pears at room temperature to ripen. Place in a closed paper bag to hasten ripening, with apples or bananas to hasten them even more. Not all pears change color when they ripen, but they will give to gentle pressure at the stem when they are ripe. Once ripe, refrigerate loose in the low-humidity drawer. Bring back to room temperature before eating for best flavor.

❅ **FREEZING:** Uncooked pears do not freeze well. They freeze best when cooked in sugar syrup. Wash, peel, core, and boil in a 40 percent syrup (see page 155) for 1 to 2 minutes. Drain, cool, and place, covered with syrup, in an airtight

container. Leave ½-in/12-mm headspace. A small piece of crumpled water-resistant paper on top will help hold the fruit down.

↻ **USE IT UP/REVIVAL:** Brown spots on peels are natural for some varieties and can be eaten.

Browning flesh after a pear is cut is simply oxidation and will not affect taste or quality. To keep pears from browning, dip them in a solution that is half water, half lemon juice.

Some pear varieties, such as Bosc and d'Anjou, remain firm and are better for cooking. Asian pears are particularly susceptible to bruising and are thus often sold in protective sleeves.

Pears that are overripe or damaged can still be used in baked goods and sauces. Pears can be substituted for apples in most recipes.

STONE FRUITS (apricots, peaches, nectarines, cherries, plums, Pluots, etc.)

▤ **REFRIGERATOR:** After ripe

◔ **AT FRESHEST:** After ripe, 3 to 7 days in refrigerator

⬒ **OPTIMAL STORAGE:** Do not wash until ready to use. If unripe, store at room temperature out of sunlight. Place in a closed paper bag to hasten ripening. Once ripe, refrigerate loose in the low-humidity drawer or in an open paper bag with nothing stacked on top. Peaches, nectarines, and apricots will become mealy if left in the refrigerator too long. Most cherries are sold already ripe, so you may want to refrigerate immediately.

✳ **FREEZING:** You have your choice with stone fruit. You can freeze them raw (whole, in halves, or in slices) or cooked. In most cases, you'll want to remove the pits. Blanch to remove the skins and dip in a lemon juice solution (1 Tbsp lemon juice in ¼ cup/60 ml water; optional) to prevent darkening. Then either (1) place directly on a baking sheet and freeze, then transfer to airtight container; (2) place in airtight container, cover with juice or 30 to 40 percent syrup (see table on page 155), then seal, leaving ½- to 1½-in/12-mm to 4-cm headspace, depending on the container; or (3) pack into containers, layering with sugar and leaving ½- to 1½-in/12-mm to 4-cm headspace.

To freeze cherries, wash, pit, dry, place separated on a baking sheet and freeze, then transfer to an airtight container.

To defrost whole fruit, place in cold water until the skins slide off. Then slice and serve. Cherries frozen whole can be soaked in a bowl of cold water. Defrost cooked preparations in the refrigerator or microwave.

↻ **USE IT UP/REVIVAL:** Remove bruises; the rest of the fruit can be used.

To prevent browning in stone fruits, toss with some lemon juice after slicing.

The outer shell of the pits can be used to infuse just about any liquid—water (for tea or sorbet), dairy (for cakes or ice cream), or liquor—with a mild fruit flavor. To make a simple syrup, bring 2 cups/240 ml water to a boil with 2 cups/200 g sugar and 1 cup/100 g pits. Let cool and refrigerate for up to 3 weeks. Enjoy in cocktails or sauces.

Inside the pits, there is a kernel that looks like an almond. This "noyau," as it's called by the French, contains the dangerous chemical hydrogen cyanide, but can be roasted and then used to impart a bitter almond (marzipan) flavor. It is used in Europe in small amounts to flavor marzipan and amaretto dishes and also to make crème de noyaux liqueur. If you want to use this part of the fruit, be sure to check a recipe from a verified source to be sure you are doing so safely. (Some of the apricots grown in the Himalayas have kernels that can be eaten raw, just like almonds, but most cannot.)

TROPICAL FRUITS
(pineapple, papaya, and mango)

▦ **REFRIGERATOR:** After ripe

◉ **AT FRESHEST:** Whole, 2 to 3 days past ripe on counter; 5 to 7 days in refrigerator

🗄 **OPTIMAL STORAGE:** If unripe, store whole on the counter at room temperature. Once ripe, store loose on a refrigerator shelf or in the low-humidity drawer. If cut, place in an airtight container. Mangoes and papayas are often already ripe when sold, in which case refrigerate immediately. Pineapples will turn gold and then almost brown, but their sugars do not increase or ripen further.

✳ **FREEZING:** Peel and cut into chunks. Place separated on a baking sheet and freeze, then transfer to an airtight container.

↻ **USE IT UP/REVIVAL:** If a fruit is bruised or damaged, refrigerate it rather than leaving it at room temperature.

Papaya seeds can be dried and used as a mildly mustardy seasoning.

Green papaya and green mango can be used in salads, eaten fresh, or pickled. Overripe mango can still be used in chutney.

Brown or black areas inside a pineapple are caused by overchilling—cut them out and enjoy the rest.

Use the scooped-out shell of pineapple as a serving bowl for fruit salads or pineapple fried rice.

Sugar Syrup for Freezing Fruits

Many fruits have better texture and flavor if packed in sugar syrup before freezing. Fruits frozen in syrup are generally best for uncooked dessert use or for pureeing into sauces and smoothies. The proportion of sugar to water depends upon the sweetness of the fruit being frozen—for most fruit, a 40-percent syrup is recommended.

To make the sugar syrup, dissolve the sugar into the water, stirring until the liquid is clear, and then refrigerate until well chilled. Pour the chilled syrup over the prepared fruit and, before sealing the container, make sure that the fruit remains submerged in the liquid by pressing a piece of parchment paper against the surface.

Type of Syrup	Sugar	Water	Yield
10% (very light)	½ cup/100 g		4½ cups/1 L
20% (light)	1 cup/200 g		4¾ cups/1.1 L
30% (medium)	1¾ cups/350 g	**+** 1 qt/960 ml	5 cups/1.2 L
40% (heavy)	2¾ cups/550 g		5⅓ cups/1.3 L
50% (very heavy)	4 cups/800 g		6 cups/1.4 L

Source: Derived from the National Center for Home Food Preservation: nchfp.uga.edu/how/freeze/syrups.html.

Vegetables

ARTICHOKES

REFRIGERATOR: Yes

AT FRESHEST: 1 week

OPTIMAL STORAGE: Do not wash until ready to use. Slice a small bit off the end of the stem and sprinkle just that end with water. Then store in an airtight container in the high-humidity drawer of the refrigerator. Cooked artichokes should be cooled completely and then stored in the refrigerator in an airtight container for up to 1 week.

FREEZING: Trim tops, rub cut surfaces with lemon to prevent browning, and boil until "al dente" in water flavored with lemon juice. Thoroughly drain upside down. Place upside down on a baking sheet and freeze, then transfer to an airtight container. Artichokes can also be blanched, with lemon juice in the water, but it can be difficult to make sure the core of large artichokes is blanched without cooking the outsides completely. Do not freeze raw.

USE IT UP/REVIVAL: Outside leaves may be bronzed due to frost. This discoloration is cosmetic only and does not affect the edibility.

Dried whole artichokes are often used in dried floral arrangements.

ASPARAGUS

REFRIGERATOR: Yes

AT FRESHEST: 3 to 5 days

OPTIMAL STORAGE: Either put bundled stalks upright in a bowl or dish with 1 in/ 2.5 cm of water and place on a refrigerator shelf (best) or wrap the cut ends in a moist paper towel and put in a breathable bag in the high-humidity drawer of the refrigerator. Asparagus toughens quickly when not chilled, so be sure to refrigerate it as quickly as possible.

FREEZING: Blanch, immerse in ice water, dry, place separated on a baking sheet to freeze, then transfer spears to an airtight container.

USE IT UP/REVIVAL: To remove the tough parts of asparagus spears, bend them until the stiff portion snaps off.

To use the woody ends that are removed, peel them and slice into small rings to use in cooking or as part of a soup.

If spears have started to wilt, soak them in cold water before cooking, and they should perk up a bit. You can also try adding 2 to 3 Tbsp sugar to the soaking water to restore the sugars it has lost.

BEETS

📷 **REFRIGERATOR:** Yes

⏱ **AT FRESHEST:** Beets, 7 to 10 days; greens, 1 to 2 days

🗄 **OPTIMAL STORAGE:** Do not wash until ready to use. Store in a breathable bag in the high-humidity drawer of the refrigerator. Separate green tops from the beets, leaving 1 in/2.5 cm inch of stem on the beet (otherwise the greens will draw moisture away from the beet). The green tops can be stored separately in a breathable bag in the high-humidity drawer and used like chard.

❄ **FREEZING:** Wash, trim off tops, cook fully (25 to 50 minutes, depending on size), cool in ice water, rub away peel, dry, slice or cube or purée, and seal into zip-top freezer bags. If beets seem overmature, freezing can magnify woodiness and is not recommended.

🔄 **USE IT UP/REVIVAL:** Beets are the main ingredient in borscht, a popular Eastern European soup.

Beet peels and shriveled beets can be used for making natural dyes—rub your hands with salt to remove any staining.

Beets can be used to make lip stain and blush.

BROCCOLI

📷 **REFRIGERATOR:** Yes

⏱ **AT FRESHEST:** 5 to 7 days

🗄 **OPTIMAL STORAGE:** Do not wash until ready to use. Refrigerate in the original wrapping or a breathable bag in the high-humidity drawer.

❄ **FREEZING:** Wash, separate into smaller florets, blanch, immerse in ice water, and drain until dry. Lay florets out separately on a baking sheet and freeze, then transfer to an airtight container.

🔄 **USE IT UP/REVIVAL:** Eat the stalks! You can grate them and make a slaw, use in a stir-fry, or just chop and cook them like the broccoli tops. Depending on use, it helps to peel off the tough outer skin. (See the Broccoli Stalk Salad recipe on page 130.)

To revive slightly limp broccoli, apply ice directly to the bunches or plunge into an ice-water bath, drain, and place in refrigerator.

BRUSSELS SPROUTS

📷 **REFRIGERATOR:** Yes

⏱ **AT FRESHEST:** 10 days

🗄 **OPTIMAL STORAGE:** Do not wash until ready to use. Store loose Brussels sprouts in a breathable bag in the high-humidity drawer of the refrigerator. Brussels sprouts on the stalk will last longer than those off the stalk—wrap the bottom of the stalk with a moist paper towel and then plastic wrap and keep it in the refrigerator, space permitting, or in a cold place.

❄ **FREEZING:** Wash, trim any yellowing outer leaves, blanch, immerse in ice water, drain until dry, and pack into an airtight container.

↻ **USE IT UP/REVIVAL:** Peel away the yellowing outer layers of sprouts; often there is still a significant and beautiful sprout inside.

Brussels sprout stalks tend to be too tough and woody to eat (though the thinner end may be tender enough). They can be used in soup stock.

CARROTS

▦ **REFRIGERATOR:** Yes

◉ **AT FRESHEST:** Carrots, 2 weeks, a few months in a root cellar environment; carrot tops, 2 days

◔ **OPTIMAL STORAGE:** Do not wash until ready to use. Store in a breathable bag in the high-humidity drawer or submerged in water on a shelf of the refrigerator. Store cut carrots in water in the refrigerator. Separate green leafy tops, if present, from the roots, leaving 1 in/2.5 cm of stem on the carrots (otherwise, the tops will draw moisture away from the carrots). The green tops can be stored in a breathable bag in the high-humidity drawer and used like fresh herbs to add color and flavor to dishes.

❄ **FREEZING:** Remove tops, wash, blanch, cool, chop or purée, and pack into an airtight container. Raw carrots can also be shredded and frozen in zip-top freezer bags and used for baking.

↻ **USE IT UP/REVIVAL:** Carrots do not need to be peeled, just washed carefully; however, peeling does remove some bitterness.

Bruised, browning, or damaged carrots can be salvaged by peeling away the external layers and removing the damaged pieces with a paring knife.

The whitish coloring that appears on cut carrots is simply dehydration.

Revive limp carrots by placing them in an ice bath in the refrigerator for 1 hour.

Limp carrots can be used in soups and stews and stocks.

Carrot tops are great additions to soups and stews, or even floral arrangements.

CAULIFLOWER

▦ **REFRIGERATOR:** Yes

◉ **AT FRESHEST:** 5 to 7 days

◔ **OPTIMAL STORAGE:** Do not wash until ready to use. Store in the original wrapping or in a breathable bag in the high-humidity drawer of the refrigerator.

❄ **FREEZING:** Wash, separate into smaller florets, blanch, immerse in ice water, drain until dry, lay florets out separately on a baking sheet to freeze, then transfer to an airtight container.

↻ **USE IT UP/REVIVAL:** A yellowish coloring on cauliflower is from exposure to sun while growing and does not affect edibility.

Brown spots that appear are normal and harmless when small and light brown in color; if the appearance is not to your liking, use it to make dips and soups.

Use the green leaves at the base of cauliflower just as you would cabbage (or just throw into whatever you're making with the cauliflower).

CELERY

REFRIGERATOR: Yes

AT FRESHEST: 2 weeks

OPTIMAL STORAGE: Refrigerate either standing in a jar with water or in a perforated or open plastic bag in the high-humidity drawer.

FREEZING: Celery loses its crispness when frozen but can be used for cooked dishes. Slice to the size you would cook with, blanch, immerse in ice water, drain until dry, and place in an airtight container to freeze.

USE IT UP/REVIVAL: Wilted celery can be revived by a 10- to 15-minute soak in ice water; serving celery on ice will also enhance its crispness.

Pitted or discolored surfaces are simply places where oxidation has occurred; they can still be eaten, or pare them away.

Celery leaves add great flavor to soups, stews, and stir-fries.

Celery bottoms can be planted. See page 100 for details.

CORN ON THE COB

REFRIGERATOR: Yes

AT FRESHEST: In the husk, 2 to 3 days; husked, 1 to 2 days

OPTIMAL STORAGE: Eat as soon as possible. (The sugars in sweet corn turn to starch rapidly.) Store in husks if possible in a warmer section (middle or upper shelf) of the refrigerator or, if husked, wrapped in damp cloths in an airtight container.

FREEZING: Remove husks. If freezing on the cob, blanch for 7 minutes; if freezing just the kernels, blanch on the cob for 4 minutes. Chill, drain, and either pack whole cobs into zip-top freezer bags or scrape kernels off the cobs and pack into airtight containers or freezer bags.

USE IT UP/REVIVAL: Corn cobs can add sweet flavor to soup stock.

Make tea or soup with the husks and silks.

Corn with dry, browned, or slightly slimy outer husks is often still good once the husks and silks are removed (but not if the corn itself has slime or mold).

CUCUMBER

REFRIGERATOR: Yes

AT FRESHEST: 1 week

OPTIMAL STORAGE: Because their ideal temperature is somewhere between room temperature and refrigeration, cucumbers can be stored in a cool place on the counter or wrapped in a damp cloth and placed in a breathable bag in the high-humidity drawer of the refrigerator. Do not store near tomatoes, apples, avocados, or bananas. They are best if used within a few days, as more time at low temperatures can damage them.

FREEZING: Not recommended.

USE IT UP/REVIVAL: Peel or cut away any damaged flesh, and serve as usual.

Slightly overripe cucumbers can be bitter, but scooping out the seeds with a spoon before using helps minimize that bitterness.

Many times the skin of the cucumber is undesirable, but the inside flesh is perfectly fine. In this case, simply peel the cucumber.

Pickle, of course!

EGGPLANT

REFRIGERATOR: No

AT FRESHEST: 1 week

OPTIMAL STORAGE: Store loose or in a breathable bag in a cool place. Refrigeration can lead to browning and off-flavors.

FREEZING: Wash, peel, slice about ⅓-in/8-mm thick, blanch with ½ cup/120 ml lemon juice per 1 gl/3.8 L water, immerse in ice water, drain, then freeze in airtight container, leaving ½-in/12-mm headspace.

USE IT UP/REVIVAL: Salt the flesh of older eggplant to remove bitterness.

GARLIC AND SHALLOTS

REFRIGERATOR: Unpeeled, no; peeled, yes

AT FRESHEST: Unpeeled, a few weeks to several months (garlic will last a bit longer); peeled, up to several weeks

OPTIMAL STORAGE: Store unpeeled garlic and shallots in a cool, dark, and dry place in a well-ventilated container such as a basket or mesh bag. Do not store in plastic. To help prevent the heads from drying out, leave the papery skin on and break off cloves as needed. If peeled, store in an airtight container in the refrigerator.

FREEZING: Peel garlic or chop shallots and store in an airtight container. Both will lose crispness when thawed but will retain most of their flavor.

USE IT UP/REVIVAL: In gardens, green garlic leaves can be used just like green onions. Similarly, if garlic grows a shoot while in storage, that can be eaten as well. Even garlic flowers are edible and have a mild flavor.

Blend garlic with basil or blanched kale stems and other ingredients to make a pesto, which can be frozen for up to 6 months.

GINGER

REFRIGERATOR: Yes

AT FRESHEST: 1 to 2 months

OPTIMAL STORAGE: Refrigerate, either unwrapped or in an airtight container, in a dark section of the refrigerator.

FREEZING: Freeze whole in an airtight container and cut off slices as needed. The texture will be slightly mushy, but the flavor is fine for adding to cooked dishes.

USE IT UP/REVIVAL: Grate fresh or frozen ginger into a mug of boiling water and enjoy as a healthful tea.

Ginger does not necessarily need to be peeled before using; if the ginger is young and the skin is very fine and clings to the root, you can skip peeling.

The rough and dry spots on ginger are not dangerous; simply cut them away (and use them in tea).

GREEN BEANS, SNAP PEAS, AND FRESH PEAS

REFRIGERATOR: Yes

AT FRESHEST: 3 to 5 days

OPTIMAL STORAGE: Green beans and peas are fragile vegetables; they quickly degrade in quality, even at cold temperatures. Store unwashed peas and beans in the refrigerator in a breathable bag in the high-humidity drawer, but try to eat them as quickly as possible.

FREEZING: Blanch, immerse in ice water, drain until dry, and then place in an airtight container.

USE IT UP/REVIVAL: If the pods are too tough to eat (this can happen when beans are overmature and bulging from the pods), peas can still be shelled and eaten or refrigerated in an airtight container and used within 2 days.

You can let the shelled peas dry out and save their seeds for planting in your garden.

Although often the ends of the beans are cut off before cooking, they need not be removed; only the stem end and enjoy the rest of the bean.

Salvage less-than-ideal green beans by removing any that are soft to the touch or slimy. Wash the remainder in cold water.

Briefly cooking older green beans can enhance their flavor.

GREEN ONIONS (scallions)

- **REFRIGERATOR:** Yes

- **AT FRESHEST:** 1 to 2 weeks

- **OPTIMAL STORAGE:** Store in a breathable bag in the high-humidity drawer of the refrigerator.

- **FREEZING:** Wash, dry, chop (if desired), and seal in zip-top freezer bags. Will lose crispness but retain flavor.

- **USE IT UP/REVIVAL:** Soak root ends in cold water for an hour to revive wilting green onions.

  Browning or dried outer layers can often be peeled away, revealing a fresh green onion that is still fine to eat.

  Grow new green onions from the sliced-off roots. See page 100 for details.

GREENS, HEARTY
(kale, chard, beet greens, bok choy, collard greens, cabbage, etc.)

- **REFRIGERATOR:** Yes

- **AT FRESHEST:** 3 to 5 days

- **OPTIMAL STORAGE:** Do not wash until ready to use. Remove twist ties and store loosely, with a damp cloth, in an airtight container in the high-humidity drawer of the refrigerator.

- **FREEZING:** Blanch, immerse in ice water, drain, dry, and then place in an airtight container.

- **USE IT UP/REVIVAL:** Soak wilted greens in a bowl of ice water for 5 to 10 minutes to revive crispness.

Kale stems can be blanched and made into a pesto. They can also be prepared right along with the leaves.

Chard stems make a great substitute for celery, particularly in cooked preparations.

GREENS, SALAD (lettuce, arugula, endive, radicchio, and spinach)

- **REFRIGERATOR:** Yes

- **AT FRESHEST:** 7 days; head lettuces, such as iceberg, keep longer than leaf lettuces

- **OPTIMAL STORAGE:** Store with a damp cloth in an airtight container in the high-humidity drawer of the refrigerator. Alternatively, place in a cup with water on the counter, as you would cut flowers. Cover bitter lettuces, such as endive, as they increase in bitterness when exposed to light.

- **FREEZING:** Not recommended.

- **USE IT UP/REVIVAL:** Heads of lettuce that appear rotten can be salvaged by removing several outer leaves and cutting away any bruised parts.

  Packaged lettuce with a few bad pieces can be saved by removing those pieces and then soaking the rest in ice water for 5 to 10 minutes.

  Wilted greens can be soaked in ice water 5 to 10 minutes to perk them up.

  Yes, lettuce can be cooked! Even older or wilted leaves and packaged mixes. See recipe on page 127.

  If the outside leaves of a bitter lettuce are too bitter, remove them and try the inner leaves, as exposure to light can increase bitterness.

HERBS, BASIL

REFRIGERATOR: No

AT FRESHEST: Up to 1 week

OPTIMAL STORAGE: Trim stem ends and stick the bunch in a tall glass of water, as you would cut flowers. Loosely cover with a plastic bag and keep on the counter, changing the water daily. It can also be stored in the refrigerator by wrapping in cloth and then placing in an airtight container on the top shelf. However, the cold is likely to brown the leaves quickly.

FREEZING: Chop and cover with olive oil or blend with olive oil in a food processor or blender. Freeze in an ice-cube tray, transferring to an airtight container or zip-top freezer bag when frozen. Basil leaves can be frozen on baking sheets and then transferred, but they may blacken. Basil can also be used to make pesto and then frozen.

USE IT UP/REVIVAL: If wilted, trim stems, then soak in ice water for 15 minutes. Both stems and flowers are edible.

HERBS OTHER THAN BASIL
(rosemary, parsley, cilantro, dill, lavender, mint, sage, thyme, etc.)

REFRIGERATOR: Yes

AT FRESHEST: 1 week, depending on the herb (heartier herbs such as rosemary and thyme last longer)

OPTIMAL STORAGE: Store loosely wrapped in a cloth in a breathable bag in the high-humidity drawer of the refrigerator.

FREEZING: For heartier herbs like rosemary, sage, thyme, and oregano, pack into ice-cube trays, filling them two-thirds full, then top the compartments with olive oil or melted butter; cover lightly and freeze, then transfer the cubes to an airtight container.

To freeze without oil, wash, drain, and pat dry with a cloth. Wrap a few sprigs or leaves in freezer wrap and put in an airtight container. The flavor of many herbs is well preserved by freezing (more so than by drying for many), but they may become discolored and limp.

Herbs can be dried in the microwave—a process that, in fact, preserves their flavor better than using ovens or dehydrators. Remove stems, place herbs between two paper towels, and microwave on High (full power) for 1 minute. If not completely dry, continue to cook and check in 20-second intervals. Stop early if you smell burning.

USE IT UP/REVIVAL: Place fresh herbs in a jar of olive oil and store in the refrigerator for a flavored oil (bring to room temperature before using within 4 days).

Strong rosemary stems can be used as skewers for kebabs.

MUSHROOMS

REFRIGERATOR: Yes

AT FRESHEST: Up to 1 week, depending on type

OPTIMAL STORAGE: Mushrooms should be used as quickly as possible after purchase. Do not wash until ready to use. Store in original packaging or in a paper bag on the lower shelf in the refrigerator. For very delicate mushrooms, lay them in a single layer on a tray and cover with a damp cloth. Don't store mushrooms next to anything strong smelling, as they tend to absorb odors (one of the reasons to use them quickly).

FREEZING: Steam or sauté and then pack into airtight containers. Do not pack raw.

USE IT UP/REVIVAL: Stems of most common mushrooms can be eaten.

Dirty mushrooms can be wiped clean with a delicate cloth.

Marinate mushrooms that are on the older side in an oil, vinegar, and herb mixture of your choice.

ONIONS

REFRIGERATOR: No

AT FRESHEST: Whole, several months; cut, 7 days

OPTIMAL STORAGE: Store whole onions in a cool, dark, dry, well-ventilated place. Do not store in plastic. Remove onions with mold or other signs of dampness immediately so others aren't affected. Storing in hanging sacks is a great idea, as it

encourages ventilation. Do not store near potatoes; onions will cause the potatoes to sprout.

Partially used onions should be stored in an airtight container in the refrigerator, with the peel left on if possible.

FREEZING: Remove the skins and root. Chop and freeze raw. Don't blanch. Plan to use in cooked dishes when thawed.

USE IT UP/REVIVAL: Onions sprouting green tops are still safe to eat; simply remove the green sprouts and peel as usual. Use the green sprout as you would a green onion.

If there are layers of onion that are bruised or rotten, peel them away until you get down to a fresh layer.

The sliced-off (and cleaned) ends of an onion can be saved and used for soup stock or can be put into a pot of cooking beans for added flavor.

Onion peels can be used to make a dye for Easter eggs or even fabric. You'll get a gold color from yellow onions and a purplish brown color from red onions. See page 103.

The sliced-off root end of an onion can be planted. See page 100.

PARSNIPS

REFRIGERATOR: Yes

AT FRESHEST: 3 to 4 weeks

OPTIMAL STORAGE: Do not wash until ready to use. Store in a breathable bag in the high-humidity drawer of the refrigerator.

FREEZING: Wash, peel and chop (if necessary, chop out the hard core), blanch, immerse in ice water, dry, and pack into an airtight container.

↻ **USE IT UP/REVIVAL:** Young parsnips and parsnips without a waxed coating do not need to be peeled, just washed well. If you scratch the peel with your fingernail and notice a waxy residue, peel the parsnip and discard the peels.

Parsnips are very sweet and can be grated and used in cakes and breads.

PEPPERS (red, green, or hot)

▦ **REFRIGERATOR:** Yes

◉ **AT FRESHEST:** Whole, 5 to 7 days; cut, 3 days

◉ **OPTIMAL STORAGE:** Do not wash until ready to use. Store in a breathable bag in the low-humidity drawer of the refrigerator. Store cut peppers in an airtight container in the refrigerator.

❋ **FREEZING:** Wash and core peppers, chop and lay out on a baking sheet to freeze, then transfer to an airtight container. Can also be blanched. Or roast peppers and then flatten them and pack into zip-top freezer bags. Best used for cooked dishes, as crispness can be lost when thawed.

↻ **USE IT UP/REVIVAL: Drying (hot peppers)**—If you have a lot, string them up together and hang in a well-ventilated place in the sun as long as the evenings don't get cool enough to cause dew. Alternatively, use a dehydrator or place in the oven at 120°F/50°C for several hours until fully dry.

Green peppers last a lot longer than red peppers, which are fully ripe when picked. All peppers start out green on the plant, then change to red or yellow, purple, etc.

POTATOES

▦ **REFRIGERATOR:** No

◉ **AT FRESHEST:** New potatoes, 2 to 3 days; mature potatoes, 2 to 3 weeks; a few months in a root cellar environment

◉ **OPTIMAL STORAGE:** Do not wash until ready to use. Store away from sunlight in a cool, dark, dry, well-ventilated place, in a bag with ventilation—mesh, paper, burlap, or perforated plastic.

❋ **FREEZING:** Not recommended. If you must, you can cook, mash, add 1 Tbsp white vinegar, and place in an airtight container.

↻ **USE IT UP/REVIVAL:** Greening potatoes should be peeled deeply or discarded, as the green can indicate natural toxins that are not destroyed by cooking; sprouts should be cut out before using potatoes.

Bruised or damaged potatoes can be salvaged by peeling away outer layers and removing rotting pieces with a paring knife.

Potato cooking water can be used to add flavor to yeast breads.

If you've oversalted a soup, cut a boiling potato into slices and add to the pot. Simmer for 5 to 10 minutes and remove the potato; it will have absorbed some of the salt.

RADISHES

📠 **REFRIGERATOR:** Yes

🌀 **AT FRESHEST:** Radishes, 1 to 2 weeks; radish greens, 2 to 3 days

🫙 **OPTIMAL STORAGE:** Do not wash until ready to use. Separate green tops from radishes (otherwise the greens will draw out moisture). Store radishes in a breathable bag in the high-humidity drawer of the refrigerator, and store the greens as you would other dark greens.

❄️ **FREEZING:** Not recommended.

🔄 **USE IT UP/REVIVAL:** Radish greens are edible and can be eaten in salad or cooked.

Peeling radishes is not necessary, but can give them a less peppery taste.

SQUASH, SUMMER
(zucchini, pattypan, crookneck)

📠 **REFRIGERATOR:** Yes

🌀 **AT FRESHEST:** 5 days

🫙 **OPTIMAL STORAGE:** Do not wash until ready to use. Store in a breathable bag in the high-humidity drawer of the refrigerator. Wrap cut ends with damp cloth. Handle carefully, as bruising can reduce vitamin content.

❄️ **FREEZING:** Wash, chop, blanch, immerse in ice water, drain, dry, and then place in an airtight container. Or shred raw zucchini and place in an airtight container.

🔄 **USE IT UP/REVIVAL:** Peel or cut away any damaged flesh, and serve as usual.

Slightly overripe squash are best served cooked. Grate overgrown squash or squash that has started to go soft for use in baked goods such as muffins and breads. Note that the grated squash can be frozen.

Summer squash can be substituted for pickles in some pickling recipes.

SQUASH, WINTER
(pumpkin, acorn, butternut, Hubbard)

📠 **REFRIGERATOR:** No

🌀 **AT FRESHEST: At 55°F/13°C**—Acorn, 1 month; pumpkin and butternut, 2 to 3 months; Hubbard, 3 to 6 months. Life may be somewhat shorter if stored on the counter at room temperature

🫙 **OPTIMAL STORAGE:** Store unwrapped in a cool, dark, dry, well-ventilated place (they keep best at around 55°F/13°C).

❄️ **FREEZING:** Cook until soft, remove rind, and mash. Allow to cool, then place in an airtight container and freeze.

🔄 **USE IT UP/REVIVAL:** The skins of most winter squash, including butternut and acorn squash, are edible when cooked.

The seeds of winter squash are also edible and can be toasted just as you would pumpkin seeds.

The skins can be used to make an edible container for other dishes—fill with desired filling, then bake and serve.

Make squash "chips" in the oven. Slice very thin using a mandoline or peeler, toss with olive oil and salt, and bake at 400°F/200°C until the chips are curling but not browned, 20 to 35 minutes. Cool for 10 minutes—they will crisp the way cookies do after coming out of oven.

SWEET POTATOES

REFRIGERATOR: No

AT FRESHEST: 1 to 2 weeks if stored at room temperature, 1 month or longer in a root cellar environment

OPTIMAL STORAGE: Do not wash until ready to use. Store in a cool, dark, dry, well-ventilated place—ideally a root cellar with temperatures of 55° to 60°F/13° to 15°C. Avoid potatoes with holes or cuts in the skin; this leads to decay that can affect the whole sweet potato.

FREEZING: Cook until almost tender, and let cool. Peel and cut in halves or slices, or mash. Dip in a solution of ½ cup/120 ml lemon juice to 1 qt/1 L water to prevent browning, or if mashing, add 2 Tbsp lemon juice per 1 qt/200 g of sweet potatoes. Place in container with ½-in/12-mm headspace and freeze. Baked sweet potatoes can also be frozen slightly undercooked and wrapped in foil, then put in a container, with final cooking completed when ready to eat.

USE IT UP/REVIVAL: Sweet potato skins are edible.

TOMATOES

REFRIGERATOR: No, unless cut

AT FRESHEST: Whole, ripe, up to 3 days at room temperature; cut or nearing over-ripe, 2 to 3 days in refrigerator

OPTIMAL STORAGE: Do not wash until ready to use. Store fresh tomatoes on the counter away from direct sunlight, with the stem end up. Storing them on their sides will cause bruising. Refrigeration can cause loss of sweetness and texture but is an option to add a few days of life if nearing overripe; cut tomatoes should be refrigerated. If refrigerating, store in their original container or in a breathable bag in the low-humidity drawer. Let come to room temperature before eating for best flavor.

FREEZING: Freeze raw or cooked in zip-top freezer bags. Frozen whole tomatoes won't have a great texture once you defrost them, but you can easily turn them into sauce or salsa or soup, where they are mashed up anyway. You can leave the skin on whole tomatoes, because it will come off under cold running water during defrosting. You can also freeze tomato juice, stewed tomatoes, tomato paste, and any tomato products, such as salsa.

USE IT UP/REVIVAL: To ripen green tomatoes, put them in a brown paper bag with a piece of ripe fruit to initiate the ripening process.

Cracked tomatoes can still be eaten. Just cut out and discard the cracked parts and enjoy the rest.

TURNIPS

REFRIGERATOR: Yes, unless there is a root cellar

AT FRESHEST: 2 weeks in refrigerator, 2 months in a root cellar environment

OPTIMAL STORAGE: Do not wash until ready to use. Separate from their green tops (otherwise the greens will draw out moisture). Store in an airtight container in the refrigerator, unless a root cellar is an option. Store the greens as you would hearty greens in the refrigerator.

FREEZING: Wash, peel and chop, blanch, cool, and pack in an airtight container.

USE IT UP/REVIVAL: Turnip greens are edible.

Turnips do not need to be peeled before eating.

Turnips can be pickled.

Meat, Poultry, and Seafood

BACON

REFRIGERATOR: Yes

AT FRESHEST: Fresh, 7 days; dry-cured, 4 to 6 days; cooked, 4 to 5 days; frozen, up to 3 months

OPTIMAL STORAGE: Original packaging or inside a zip-top plastic bag with air removed.

FREEZING: Unopened—Overwrap store package with heavy-duty foil.
Opened—Layer slices between wax or parchment paper, and then wrap tightly a few times with the paper; store in a sealed zip-top freezer bag.

USE IT UP/REVIVAL: Bacon s'mores, bacon cookies, bacon bits, bacon-wrapped vegetables, bacon cupcakes . . .
Store bacon grease in a covered container in the refrigerator and, when the mood strikes, use it in cooking. Try rubbing bacon fat onto cleaned russet potatoes before baking; meanwhile, sauté some red onions in bacon fat, then top the potatoes with the onions and crumble on some cooked bacon if you've got it.

CANNED FISH

REFRIGERATOR: Once opened

AT FRESHEST: Unopened, 3 years; opened, 3 to 4 days; frozen, up to 2 months

OPTIMAL STORAGE: Unopened—Cool, dry place.
Opened—Covered in an airtight container (not the original can) in the refrigerator.

FREEZING: Remove from the can and place in an airtight container or zip-top freezer bag.

USE IT UP/REVIVAL: Feed small amounts to your dog or cat.
Discard cans that are dented, leaking, bulging, or rusted.
Make a tuna melt or a tuna casserole.

CANNED MEAT

REFRIGERATOR: Once opened (unless label says to store refrigerated)

AT FRESHEST: Unopened, 2 years; opened, 3 to 4 days; frozen, 1 to 2 months

OPTIMAL STORAGE: Unopened—Cool, dry place.
Opened—Covered in an airtight container (not the original can) in the refrigerator.

※ **FREEZING:** Remove from the can and place in an airtight container or zip-top freezer bag.

↻ **USE IT UP/REVIVAL:** Discard cans that are dented, leaking, bulging, or rusted.

Make a "Spamburger" with pineapple, add some Spam to your macaroni and cheese, make some Spam and kimchi fried rice . . .

DELI MEATS

▤ **REFRIGERATOR:** Yes

◉ **AT FRESHEST:** Unopened, 2 weeks; opened, 3 to 5 days; frozen, 1 to 2 months

◙ **OPTIMAL STORAGE:** Store prepackaged meat in original packaging; for meat that is not prepackaged, keep in an airtight container in either the shallow meat drawer or the lowest shelf of the refrigerator.

※ **FREEZING:** Keep in original packaging or wrap tightly in heavy-duty plastic wrap or freezer paper and then again in heavy-duty aluminum foil. Thaw in the refrigerator.

↻ **USE IT UP/REVIVAL:** Deli meat can be eaten after the "sell by" date, but it's not a good idea to eat it cold after the "use by" or "best by" date. If it is past that date and still smells and appears fine, cook it thoroughly before eating.

Cooked deli meat makes a great breakfast accompaniment for eggs. For some cuts, when a whole slice is cooked, it will form a cup shape that can then act as a "basket" for the eggs.

FRESH FISH

▤ **REFRIGERATOR:** Yes

◉ **AT FRESHEST:** **Fresh**— Raw, 1 to 2 days; cooked, 3 to 4 days; frozen raw, 2 to 6 months (lean fish keeps longer); frozen cooked, 4 to 6 months **Smoked**—2 weeks; frozen, 2 months

◙ **OPTIMAL STORAGE:** Remove from package, remove any guts, and pat dry with paper towels. Place on a cake rack set in a shallow pan for up to 24 hours; fill the pan with crushed ice if it will be stored more than 24 hours. Do not allow ice to come directly into contact with the fish. Cover the pan with plastic wrap or foil, seal tightly, and refrigerate. Each day, rinse the fish under cold water, clean the rack and pan, and change the ice. Smoked fish should be stored in an airtight container on the lowest shelf of the refrigerator.

※ **FREEZING:** Pat dry with paper towels. Wrap tightly in plastic wrap, squeezing out all the air, then wrap tightly in aluminum foil and freeze. Thaw in the refrigerator.

↻ **USE IT UP/REVIVAL:** Fish heads can be used to make fish soup or bouillabaisse. They're also used in several Asian dishes, such as curries.

Fish tacos are a great way to use up leftover fish.

FRESH MEAT
(poultry, pork, beef, lamb)

REFRIGERATOR: Yes

AT FRESHEST: Poultry, whole cuts—
Raw, 1 to 2 days; cooked, 3 to 4 days;
frozen raw, 9 to 12 months; frozen cooked,
3 to 4 months

    Pork, whole cuts—Raw, 3 to 5 days;
cooked, 4 to 5 days; frozen raw, 4 to
6 months; frozen cooked, 2 to 3 months

    Beef, whole cuts—Raw, 3 to 5 days;
cooked, 4 to 5 days; frozen raw, 6 to
12 months, depending on cut; frozen
cooked, 2 to 3 months

    Lamb, whole cuts—Raw, 1 to 2 days;
cooked, 4 to 5 days; frozen raw, 9 months;
frozen cooked, 2 to 3 months

    Ground meats—Fresh, 1 to 2 days;
frozen, 3 to 4 months

OPTIMAL STORAGE: Store on the bottom
shelf of the refrigerator, wrapped tightly
in airtight packaging (it's best to leave
it in the store packaging until first use).
Place on a tray if there is a chance of
dripping. The longer meat is left warmer
than refrigerated temperatures, the more
quickly it will spoil. Therefore, shop for it
last and go directly home to put it away,
if possible. Alternatively, keep a cooler in
your car. Freeze unless you plan to use it
within a couple of days. Poultry should not
be rinsed before use. Cooked meat should
be stored in airtight containers.

FREEZING: Divide meat into meal-size
portions. If freezing for a short period, one
layer of wrapping is sufficient. If freezing
for longer than 2 months, wrap in a second
layer to prevent freezer burn. The original
packaging is often not moisture proof. It's
preferable to rewrap more tightly so that
the meat is exposed to less air. If leaving
in original packaging, overwrap tightly
with heavy-duty foil or freezer paper, or
place in a zip-top freezer bag and remove
the air. If repackaging, separate portions
with freezer paper, wrap again tightly in
freezer paper, then place in an airtight
container or a zip-top freezer bag with the
air removed. An additional layer of heavy-
duty foil before putting the wrapped meat
in the container is optional and may help
if it will be stored for a long period. Thaw
in an ice-water bath, a microwave, or
the refrigerator. See page 57 for further
directions on safe thawing practices.

USE IT UP/REVIVAL: Portions with freezer
burn are not harmful but may be dry and
tasteless. If desired, cut out those areas
and discard; the rest can be eaten.

    Bones can be used to make stock or
add flavor to beans. See page 96 on feeding bones to pets.

HOT DOGS AND PRECOOKED SAUSAGE

REFRIGERATOR: Yes

AT FRESHEST: Unopened, 2 weeks; opened,
7 days; frozen, 1 to 2 months

OPTIMAL STORAGE: Store on the the bottom
shelf of the refrigerator, wrapped tightly
in airtight packaging. (Even though they're
precooked, make sure to heat the sausages thoroughly before consuming.)

* **FREEZING:** Unopened vacuum-packed packages can be stored directly in freezer; otherwise double-wrap tightly in freezer paper or plastic wrap.

↻ **USE IT UP/REVIVAL:** Extra sausages are great in soups and chili.

SAUSAGE (fresh and dry/cured; see "Hot Dogs" for precooked)

▦ **REFRIGERATOR:** Yes

◉ **AT FRESHEST: Fresh**—Uncooked, unopened, 1 to 2 days; open, 1 to 2 days; cooked, 3 to 4 days; frozen, 1 to 2 months
Dry/cured—Unopened, 6 months in pantry or indefinitely in refrigerator; opened, 3 weeks in refrigerator; frozen, 1 to 2 months

⊖ **OPTIMAL STORAGE:** Store on the bottom shelf of the refrigerator, wrapped tightly in airtight packaging.

* **FREEZING:** Wrap tightly in plastic, and then wrap in white freezer paper.

↻ **USE IT UP/REVIVAL:** Combine cooked sausage with rice and spices to make a version of jambalaya, or make stuffed peppers with the mixture.

SHELLFISH

▦ **REFRIGERATOR:** Yes

◉ **AT FRESHEST:** Fresh, 1 to 2 days; shucked, 2 days; cooked, 1 to 2 days; frozen, up to 4 months

⊖ **OPTIMAL STORAGE: Live**—Place in a bowl on the low shelf in the refrigerator and keep damp with a cloth, but do not allow to come into direct contact with ice or water (for live lobster and crab, store in moist packaging such as seaweed or damp paper towels). Do not store live shellfish in airtight containers or bags, since the animals can die from lack of oxygen. Do not store beneath raw meat, to avoid contamination.
Shrimp—Keep in their own containers or in a zip-top bag on a bed of ice in refrigerator. Do not allow ice to come in direct contact with the seafood. Eat as soon as possible.

* **FREEZING:** Live oysters can be frozen live; just wash the shells and place in a plastic zip-top freezer bag. Alternatively, wash the oyster shells, and shuck into a strainer (save the liquor). Rinse to remove sand. Place oysters and liquor in a plastic container or zip-top freezer bag, leaving ½-in/12-mm headspace; seal; and freeze. Do not freeze dead oysters (with open shells). For shrimp, wash and drain, freeze raw with heads removed but shells still on. Package in zip-top freezer bags, leaving ¼-in/6-mm headspace; seal and freeze.

↻ **USE IT UP/REVIVAL:** Do not eat shellfish such as oysters or mussels that have died before shucking (not even if you cook them).
Pulverize oyster shells with a hammer (best to boil the shells and let dry first), then sprinkle around the garden to deter slugs. Oyster shells can also be fed to chickens.
Crab pincers can double as little picks to get the leg meat out of the shell.

Pantry Staples

BREAD

REFRIGERATOR: No

AT FRESHEST: Counter, a few days; freezer, 6 months

OPTIMAL STORAGE: If using bread within 2 days, store at room temperature in a bread box or paper bag to reduce moisture loss while allowing the crust to remain crisp. Do not keep at room temperature in a plastic bag, as this encourages mold. If using beyond 2 days, freeze individual slices, if that's how you plan to use it. Keep in the refrigerator, well wrapped, only if you plan to toast it.

FREEZING: Wrap tightly in airtight wrapping. Thaw at room temperature or put directly in the toaster or oven.

USE IT UP/REVIVAL: As long as it's not too old, staling can be reversed by toasting or reheating at about 140°F/60°C.

There are myriad recipes for using stale bread—bread pudding, French toast, bread crumbs, and croutons are some of the most common. Gazpacho uses stale bread as well. See page 126 for a recipe.

BREAD CRUMBS

REFRIGERATOR: Not necessarily

AT FRESHEST: Commercial, in pantry, 1 year; fresh, in refrigerator, 1 month; fresh, in freezer, 1 year

OPTIMAL STORAGE: Airtight container in a cool, dry place.

FREEZING: Airtight container.

USE IT UP/REVIVAL: Discard if moldy. Use bread crumbs as a filler to make meatloaf, hamburgers, or veggie burgers.

FLOUR, WHITE

REFRIGERATOR: Not necessary

AT FRESHEST: Pantry, 1 year; refrigerator, 2 years

OPTIMAL STORAGE: Opaque, airtight container in a cool, dry, dark place. For longer storage, place in the refrigerator (bring to room temperature before using). In all cases, store away from foods with strong odors.

FREEZING: Store in an airtight container or zip-top freezer bag. Bring to room temperature before using.

↻ **USE IT UP/REVIVAL:** Use up your flour by making a pie crust or cookie dough and freeze it for up to 3 months.

Polish copper or brass! Combine equal parts flour, salt, and white vinegar and apply the mixture with a sponge to brass or copper, let dry, then rinse with warm water and buff dry with a cloth.

FLOUR, WHOLE WHEAT

▦ **REFRIGERATOR:** Yes; freezer recommended

◔ **AT FRESHEST:** Opened, in refrigerator, 6 to 8 months; freezer, 2 years

⊙ **OPTIMAL STORAGE:** Opaque, airtight, moisture-proof container in the refrigerator or freezer away from foods with strong odors.

✳ **FREEZING:** Store in an airtight container or zip-top freezer bag. Bring to room temperature before using.

↻ **USE IT UP/REVIVAL:** Old whole-wheat flour won't make you ill, but it can go rancid. In order to tell, taste a tiny amount. If it has a strongly bitter taste, it's likely rancid. Otherwise, it should still be fine to use.

Substituting half the required amount of white flour with wheat flour can make any recipe more healthful.

OATS

▦ **REFRIGERATOR:** Optional

◔ **AT FRESHEST:** 1 year

⊙ **OPTIMAL STORAGE:** Airtight container in a dry, dark, cool place, or freeze in an airtight container.

✳ **FREEZING:** Airtight container.

↻ **USE IT UP/REVIVAL:** Leftover oatmeal can be used to make bread and pancakes, or can be fried into oatmeal cakes.

Dried or cooked oats add heartiness and flavor to smoothies.

PASTA

▦ **REFRIGERATOR:** All fresh and cooked pasta should be refrigerated; keep dry pasta in the pantry.

◔ **AT FRESHEST:** Dried, pantry, 2 years; fresh, in refrigerator, 2 days; cooked, in refrigerator, 3 to 5 days; fresh, in freezer, 2 months

⊙ **OPTIMAL STORAGE:** Store dry pasta in original packaging or an airtight container; wrap fresh pasta in airtight wrapping.

✳ **FREEZING:** Wrap fresh pasta tightly in airtight wrapping or seal into a zip-top bag. Freezing cooked pasta may alter its texture, so it's best used in a casserole or baked dish when thawed.

↻ **USE IT UP/REVIVAL:** Bake up a pasta dish in a foil-lined pan, then allow to cool and place, covered with parchment paper, in freezer until frozen. Remove the pasta dish from the pan, wrap in more foil, then seal into a zip-top freezer bag. Keep for up to 2 months; thaw in the refrigerator overnight and pop back into the pan and place in the oven to warm through.

Make pasta salad. See recipe page 129.

Dried pasta is great for all sorts of children's crafts.

QUINOA

REFRIGERATOR: No

AT FRESHEST: 1 year

OPTIMAL STORAGE: Airtight container in a dry, dark, cool place, or freeze.

FREEZING: Airtight container.

USE IT UP/REVIVAL: Bake uncooked quinoa into cookies for an added crunch.

Leftover cooked quinoa? Make a flourless chocolate cake!

RICE, BROWN AND WILD

REFRIGERATOR: Yes

AT FRESHEST: 6 to 12 months; cooked, 1 week

OPTIMAL STORAGE: Airtight container in the refrigerator. Brown rice will eventually go rancid because of the oils in its outer hull; this happens more quickly when stored in a pantry.

FREEZING: Cook, cool, spread flat inside large zip-top freezer bags, and squeeze out the air. Pack the bags into an airtight container or larger bag.

USE IT UP/REVIVAL: To soften leftover cooked rice that has hardened, add a small amount of water and heat gently.

Extra cooked rice can be used to make homemade rice cakes, rice salads, and fried rice (see recipe on page 128).

RICE, WHITE

REFRIGERATOR: No

AT FRESHEST: Indefinitely; cooked, 1 week

OPTIMAL STORAGE: Airtight container in a dry, dark, cool place. Cooked rice should be stored in an airtight container in the refrigerator.

FREEZING: Cook, cool, spread flat inside large freezer bags, and squeeze out air. Pack the bags into an airtight container or larger bag.

USE IT UP/REVIVAL: To soften leftover cooked rice that has hardened, add a small amount of water and heat gently.

White rice is more shelf stable than brown rice, which is why it was originally invented. Ancient people hulled rice kernels to remove the outer layer that causes rancidity. Without that hull, rice won't go bad nearly as soon, but it isn't as nutritious.

SUGAR, BROWN

REFRIGERATOR: No

AT FRESHEST: Indefinitely

OPTIMAL STORAGE: Opaque, airtight, moisture-proof container in a cool location.

FREEZING: Necessary only if storing for a very long time or in a very dry area.

Place in an airtight container. Thaw for 2 to 3 hours. If ice crystals form after long freezer storage, gently stir the sugar as soon as it thaws to prevent pockets of moisture from causing damage.

↻ **USE IT UP/REVIVAL:** Brown sugar hardens easily. To soften hardened brown sugar, place in a bowl with a slice of bread, an apple slice, or a couple of damp paper towels. Cover tightly, and let sit for about 2 days. Remove the bread or apple or towels after the sugar absorbs the moisture and softens. Stir the sugar with a fork. To soften more quickly, remove from the package and pour into an oven-safe container. Place in a 250°F/120°C oven. As soon as it's soft, measure out the amount you'll need, as it will quickly harden. Use caution, because it will be very hot.

SUGAR, WHITE

▦ **REFRIGERATOR:** No

◉ **AT FRESHEST:** Indefinitely

◙ **OPTIMAL STORAGE:** Opaque, airtight, moisture-proof container in a cool, dry location.

❄ **FREEZING:** Not recommended.

↻ **USE IT UP/REVIVAL:** To soften granulated sugar that has caked together, preheat oven to the lowest temperature. Remove the sugar from the package and put in an oven-safe container that will hold the sugar. Place in the warm oven for approximately 15 minutes. Tap the sugar with a spoon. If it starts to fall apart, turn off the oven and leave the sugar in the oven for 1 to 2 hours to completely dry out.

WHOLE GRAINS (wheat berries, spelt, uncooked popcorn, millet, amaranth, buckwheat, barley, dried corn, teff)

▦ **REFRIGERATOR:** No

◉ **AT FRESHEST:** 6 to 12 months

◙ **OPTIMAL STORAGE:** Airtight container in a dry, dark, cool place, or freeze in an airtight container.

❄ **FREEZING:** Airtight container.

↻ **USE IT UP/REVIVAL:** Whole grains are great in kids' craft projects, such as gluing different grains onto paper to make a mosaic art piece.

Make a garland of popped popcorn for your trees; the birds will love it.

Make a popcorn ball to prolong the life of popcorn that you've popped.

Dairy and Eggs

BUTTER

REFRIGERATOR: Yes

AT FRESHEST: Opened, about 3 weeks; unopened, 2 months; freezer, up to 9 months

OPTIMAL STORAGE: Keep reserves in the freezer. Butter can be kept at room temperature if it will be used up within several days, but only if kept out of the light. If used only occasionally, store in the refrigerator in its original packaging and in the cooler parts of the refrigerator (the top and middle shelves near the back). Butter readily absorbs strong odors and flavors from its surroundings; additional wrapping or storing in a closed container (bag or butter dish) can help prevent this.

Clarified butter or "ghee" keeps three times longer than other butters because the milk solids (which cause butter rancidity) have been removed. Clarified butter is good for cooking but not for use as a spread. It will keep, covered, in the refrigerator for up to 3 months.

FREEZING: For the best results, freeze fresh butter in its original carton within a zip-top freezer bag.

USE IT UP/REVIVAL: The translucent dark yellow patches on the surface of butter are simply spots that have been exposed to air and dried out. Eat them or scrape off.

Save butter wrappers to grease pans or separate homemade burger patties. Store each wrapper, folded onto itself, in the freezer in an airtight container, and use as needed.

CHEESE, HARD

REFRIGERATOR: Yes

AT FRESHEST: 1 to 10 months, depending on the cheese

OPTIMAL STORAGE: Buy small amounts of cheese. Cheese is best stored loosely wrapped in wax paper or parchment paper to allow it to breathe, which likely means rewrapping it once you get it home to get it out of plastic wrapping. Wrapping it tightly in plastic traps moisture, thus encouraging growth of bacteria and mold. Store in the refrigerator drawer, if possible, to reduce the chance that the cheese will absorb other flavors. For best taste, allow to warm to room temperature before serving (unless it's extremely warm out).

* **FREEZING:** Grate or cube before freezing, then seal into a zip-top freezer bag. Thaw in the refrigerator and use soon thereafter; the texture may be compromised, so plan to use for cooking and baking rather than straight eating.

↻ **USE IT UP/REVIVAL:** If hard cheese develops a blue-green mold on the exterior, remove ½ in/12 mm below the mold; the remainder will be fine.

Use rinds of hard cheeses to flavor soups and stews.

CHEESE, SOFT

▦ **REFRIGERATOR:** Yes

◷ **AT FRESHEST:** 1 to 4 weeks, depending on the cheese

◖ **OPTIMAL STORAGE:** Buy small amounts of cheese. Cheese is best stored loosely wrapped in wax paper or parchment paper to allow it to breathe, which likely means rewrapping it once you get it home to get it out of plastic wrapping. Wrapping it tightly in plastic traps moisture, thus encouraging growth of bacteria and mold. Store in the refrigerator drawer, if possible, to reduce the chance of the cheese absorbing other flavors. Strong-smelling cheeses should be wrapped and placed in an airtight container to avoid having their flavor absorbed into other foods. For best taste, allow to warm to room temperature before serving (unless it's extremely warm out).

* **FREEZING:** Cheese can be frozen but may become crumbly and lose flavor, and is therefore best used in cooking when

thawed. Cube before freezing for ease of use. Very soft cheeses such as Brie will not freeze all that well.

↻ **USE IT UP/REVIVAL:** Soft cheeses with blue or green molds (that are not intentional as in blue cheese) should be discarded.

Take care with unpasteurized cheeses, which carry food safety risks and are not recommended for populations at higher risk for foodborne illness.

Rinds of soft cheeses can often be eaten.

Whip small amounts of leftover soft cheeses together with some olive oil to create a delicious whipped cheese dip.

COTTAGE CHEESE

▦ **REFRIGERATOR:** Yes

◷ **AT FRESHEST:** Unopened, up to 10 days; opened, 7 days

◖ **OPTIMAL STORAGE:** Closed container in the refrigerator.

* **FREEZING:** Not recommended, although dishes that include cottage cheese as an ingredient may be frozen.

↻ **USE IT UP/REVIVAL:** Substitute for ricotta cheese in lasagna.

Cottage cheese can be used in place of cream cheese or ricotta cheese in dips, casseroles, pancakes, and desserts. Process in a blender if you prefer a smoother texture.

Add cottage cheese to custards, pasta sauces, egg dishes, cheesecakes, and all sorts of recipes where cheese or milk would normally be used.

EGGS

REFRIGERATOR: Yes

AT FRESHEST: Fresh, 3 to 5 weeks after sell-by date; freezer, 12 months; hard-boiled, 1 week.

OPTIMAL STORAGE: Keep in a cold part of the refrigerator in their original carton (not in the door, even if there's a space for them—it is too warm).

FREEZING: Eggs should not be frozen in their shells. Lightly beaten eggs can be frozen in an airtight container, with 1-in/2.5-cm headspace, or sealed in a zip-top bag with as much air removed as possible. Yolks can be frozen alone if mixed with 1 tsp salt per 1 pt/480 ml, and whites can be frozen without salt.

USE IT UP/REVIVAL: Cracked eggs should be placed into a clean, airtight container and used within 2 days. If you're not sure when it cracked, it's best to discard the egg. As eggs age, the whites will thin and the yolks will flatten, but the nutritional value will not diminish. Older egg whites are actually better for whipping up into a voluminous meringue than fresh egg whites.

Egg grades (such as A and AA) are a reflection of how well the yolk and white hold together and the appearance of the shells, not size or flavor.

Frittatas make quick work of extra eggs (and anything else in your fridge). See the recipe on page 122.

EGG SUBSTITUTES

REFRIGERATOR: Yes

AT FRESHEST: Fresh, unopened, 10 days; opened, 3 days; frozen, 12 months; thawed, 7 days

OPTIMAL STORAGE: Store in a cold part of the refrigerator, sealed in the original container. If the original container is not airtight once opened, transfer to an airtight container to extend life.

FREEZING: Freeze in the original unopened package. Freeze portions in zip-top bags with the air removed. Once thawed, do not refreeze.

USE IT UP/REVIVAL: Egg substitutes can be used just as you'd use traditional eggs, so if you're nearing the expiration of your egg substitute, bake up some cookies or make a seasonal frittata.

MILK

REFRIGERATOR: Yes (if in shelf-stable carton, refrigerate after opening)

AT FRESHEST: Pasteurized, 1 week beyond sell-by date, freezer, 3 months; shelf-stable carton, unopened, 6 months; opened, 7 to 10 days

OPTIMAL STORAGE: Keep milk in a cold part of the refrigerator (not the door), closed in its original container. It keeps its flavor better in opaque, sealable containers. Milk that comes in a shelf-stable carton has gone through ultrahigh-temperature pasteurization and can be stored in the pantry until opened, then refrigerated.

✳ **FREEZING:** Milk can be frozen, but it will separate if left frozen for long periods. Low-fat and nonfat milk separate less than whole milk. Thawed milk is best for cooking or baking purposes. Freeze in airtight containers, leaving 1-in/2.5-cm headspace. You can also freeze it in ice-cube trays, then seal the frozen cubes in a zip-top freezer bag. Thaw in the refrigerator. Do not freeze again once thawed.

↻ **USE IT UP/REVIVAL:** Sour milk can still be used in all sorts of recipes, such as baked goods, pancakes, homemade cottage cheese, cream fillings, etc. See the recipe for Sour Milk Pancakes on page 121.

Milk will smell or taste bad before it would make you sick, making a sniff test a good method for evaluation.

Do not return unused milk to the original container. Store it in its own airtight container instead.

A nomadic Asian people used to ferment milk into an alcoholic drink called *koumiss*, described by Marco Polo as having "the qualities and flavor of white wine."

MILK SUBSTITUTES (almond, soy, rice)

▦ **REFRIGERATOR:** Yes. If in shelf-stable carton, refrigerate only once opened.

◉ **AT FRESHEST:** Shelf-stable carton, unopened, up to 12 months; refrigerated packaging, unopened, 7 to 10 days; all packaging, once opened, 5 to 7 days

◐ **OPTIMAL STORAGE:** In the pantry, store in a cool, dry spot. Once in the refrigerator, store sealed in the original carton in the middle of the refrigerator, where the temperatures are not too warm or too cold.

✳ **FREEZING:** Freeze for cooking or baking purposes. Freeze in airtight containers, leaving 1-in/2.5-cm headspace. You can also freeze in ice-cube trays, then seal the frozen cubes into a zip-top freezer bag. Thaw in the refrigerator. Do not freeze again once thawed.

↻ **USE IT UP/REVIVAL:** Milk substitutes are great in place of milk in most recipes, so if you're nearing or just past the expiration date, make a smoothie or pancakes or pudding.

YOGURT

▦ **REFRIGERATOR:** Yes

◉ **AT FRESHEST:** Unopened, 2 to 3 weeks; opened, 10 days or more

◐ **OPTIMAL STORAGE:** Covered in original container in the refrigerator.

✳ **FREEZING:** Freeze to use for cooking or baking purposes. Freeze in airtight containers, leaving 1-in/2.5-cm headspace. Thaw in the refrigerator. Do not freeze again once thawed.

↻ **USE IT UP/REVIVAL:** Substitute yogurt for milk, cream, sour cream, or buttermilk in baking; just add ½ tsp baking soda per 1 cup/240 ml of yogurt added.

Drain fresh yogurt overnight in cheesecloth to make "yogurt cheese," which is thicker than regular yogurt and can be used as a spread, etc. Then use the liquid whey in smoothies.

Beans, Nuts, and Vegetarian Proteins

BEANS, CANNED OR COOKED

🗄 **REFRIGERATOR:** Yes, after opened or cooked

◎ **AT FRESHEST:** Can in pantry, several years; cooked beans, refrigerator, 3 to 5 days; freezer, up to 3 months

🫙 **OPTIMAL STORAGE:** Store cooked beans in their cooking liquid or water in an airtight container.

❋ **FREEZING:** Freeze in sealed airtight containers in their cooking liquid or water.

↻ **USE IT UP/REVIVAL:** Made too many beans? Cooked beans can also be used in all sorts of recipes, such as cookies and cakes. See page 139 for Sneaky Black Bean Brownies.

BEANS, DRY

🗄 **REFRIGERATOR:** No

◎ **AT FRESHEST:** Can last indefinitely, but after 1 year may need slightly longer cooking times

🫙 **OPTIMAL STORAGE:** Store in airtight containers in a cool, dark, dry place. Do not wash until just before use.

❋ **FREEZING:** Not recommended.

↻ **USE IT UP/REVIVAL:** If the lengthy preparation time is the reason that bag of beans is hanging around in your pantry, you might like to know that pressure cooking vastly decreases the time to cook beans. Beans soaked for as little as 1 hour will cook in 3 to 14 minutes, depending on their variety, size, and age, using a pressure cooker.

If you don't have a pressure cooker, beans can be partially cooked in the microwave to decrease conventional cooking time.

Be careful to fully cook red kidney beans, as they can be toxic when undercooked, and do not cook them in a slow cooker unless boiled for at least 10 minutes beforehand.

Do not add salt, lemon juice, vinegar, tomatoes, chili sauce, ketchup, molasses, or wine until *after* the beans are fully cooked, as they can prevent beans from becoming tender.

Brown foam in a pot of cooking beans is protein from the beans, not dirt. If you don't like this, simply skim it off or add a bit of butter or oil to the water to prevent foaming.

PEANUTS

REFRIGERATOR: Recommended

AT FRESHEST: Unopened jar in pantry, 2 years; unopened bag in pantry, 1 to 2 months; refrigerator, 4 to 6 months; freezer, 9 to 12 months. Peanuts in the shell keep longer.

OPTIMAL STORAGE: Store in a cool, dry, dark place in an airtight container. If using only occasionally, it's best to refrigerate or freeze them.

FREEZING: Shell and seal in zip-top freezer bags, or boil whole peanuts in a brine solution, drain, and seal in freezer bags.

USE IT UP/REVIVAL: Peanut soup is a popular African dish.

Peanut shells can be used to make finger puppets or ornaments or to replace Styrofoam packing peanuts. However, many folks have allergies to peanuts, so be careful with how you use the shells.

SEEDS
(pumpkin, flaxseed, sunflower)

REFRIGERATOR: Yes, ideally

AT FRESHEST: Sunflower seeds— Raw, at least 1 year at room temperature; roasted, 8 months in refrigerator, 4 months at room temperature

Flaxseeds—Whole, at least 1 year at room temperature; ground, at least 90 days in refrigerator

Pumpkin seeds—Raw, 4 to 6 months in refrigerator

OPTIMAL STORAGE: Make sure the seeds are dry before storing. Store in airtight containers in the refrigerator or at least in a cool, dark, dry place. If using only occasionally, store in the freezer (not necessary for sunflower seeds).

FREEZING: Pack into zip-top freezer bags or airtight containers.

USE IT UP/REVIVAL: If seeds are raw, they can likely be sprouted by soaking in water overnight and then leaving in aerated containers and rinsing once a day.

If moths have gotten into a container of seeds, discard all the seeds and wash the container well before using again.

TEMPEH

REFRIGERATOR: Yes

AT FRESHEST: Unopened, 10 days; opened, 3 to 4 days

OPTIMAL STORAGE: Store in original packaging until opened, an airtight container after opening.

FREEZING: Store in original packaging.

USE IT UP/REVIVAL: The black spots on tempeh and the white material between the beans are both molds that are part of the fermentation process and entirely edible (and necessary for making the tempeh).

Do not eat if slimy.

TOFU

REFRIGERATOR: Yes

AT FRESHEST: 10 days

OPTIMAL STORAGE: Refrigerate in original package until opened. Once opened, keep submerged in water in an airtight container in the refrigerator and change the water daily.

FREEZING: Freezing tofu causes moisture to drain from it and changes its consistency, making it more firm and dense. This is helpful for marinating but may not be desired for some uses. If marinating, rinse, drain, and place in a sealed zip-top freezer bag. Thaw in the refrigerator and drain, squeezing out excess moisture.

USE IT UP/REVIVAL: The consistency of frozen tofu once it's thawed makes it a great substitute for ground beef, perfect for soups, chilis, and sauces.

Make a tofu "ricotta" as a nondairy substitute for pizzas and lasagnas.

TREE NUTS (almonds, walnuts, pecans, pine nuts, pistachios)

REFRIGERATOR: Yes

AT FRESHEST: Without shell—Almonds, walnuts, pecans, pistachios in refrigerator, 1 to 2 years; freezer, 2 years or more
With shell—Almonds, walnuts, pecans (storing pistachios in the shell is not recommended), 1½ to 2 years
Pine nuts—refrigerated, 3 months; freezer, 9 months

OPTIMAL STORAGE: Wait to shell or chop until ready to use. Store shelled nuts, even if roasted, in an opaque, airtight container in the refrigerator or freezer. If you must keep them in the pantry, store in a cool, dark place in an airtight container and use within a few months. Store pine nuts tightly wrapped in plastic wrap in an airtight container.

FREEZING: Pack into tinted zip-top freezer bags and freeze.

USE IT UP/REVIVAL: Translucency or darkening can be a sign that nuts are becoming rancid. Be sure to taste before using.

Oils, Condiments, and Spices

COCONUT MILK (canned)

- **REFRIGERATOR:** Yes, once opened

- **AT FRESHEST:** Opened, 4 to 6 days

- **OPTIMAL STORAGE:** Store in a covered airtight container. Do not store metal cans in the refrigerator or freezer.

- **FREEZING:** Coconut milk can be frozen, but its consistency may change. Use frozen coconut milk for smoothies or other dishes that don't rely on its consistency. Freeze in zip-top freezer bags or in ice-cube trays, then pack frozen cubes into a freezer bag.

- **USE IT UP/REVIVAL:** Coconut milk has many recommended beauty uses, such as hair conditioner, and moisturizer when added to bath water.

COFFEE

- **REFRIGERATOR:** No

- **AT FRESHEST:** Room temperature, up to 2 weeks; freezer, 1 month

- **OPTIMAL STORAGE:** Purchase only as much coffee as you will use within two weeks to experience it at its top quality. Store in an airtight glass or ceramic container in a dark, cool location. If purchased in larger quantities, freeze a portion of it.

- **FREEZING:** Wrap weekly portions in zip-top freezer bags. Putting coffee back in the freezer once it's been taken out is not recommended because the change in temperature (and thus moisture) destroys its integrity.

- **USE IT UP/REVIVAL:** Coffee beans that are past their prime can be put into the bottom of vases of flowers or underneath tealights in votive holders as decoration.

  Place an open bowl of coffee beans in your refrigerator to reduce unwanted odors (do not plan on using the beans to make coffee to drink after this).

  Rub your hands with coffee grounds to reduce lingering odors of garlic, salmon, and cilantro.

Used coffee grounds can be turned into soil as fertilizer (in small amounts), or used to scour caked pans. It can also be used to dye paper: Pour hot coffee into a 9-by-13-in/23-by-33-cm glass container, and soak up to three pieces of paper at a time; allow to dry fully.

HONEY

▦ **REFRIGERATOR:** No

◉ **AT FRESHEST:** A few years

◎ **OPTIMAL STORAGE:** Store in a sealed container away from direct sunlight in a cool, dark, dry place (as cold as 50°F/10°C). Storing honey in the refrigerator accelerates crystallization.

✳ **FREEZING:** Store in an airtight container.

↻ **USE IT UP/REVIVAL:** Crystallized or granulated honey is still good! To reliquefy, take off the lid and place the container upright in a pan of warm water for 10 to 20 minutes, stirring occasionally. If it's in a plastic container, it's best to place it in a glass container before heating in the water. If not possible, be sure that the water is only warm and not hot to avoid any negative effects from heating plastic.

MAPLE SYRUP

▦ **REFRIGERATOR:** Yes, once opened

◉ **AT FRESHEST:** Room temperature, unopened, 2 years; refrigerator, open, 1 year; freezer, indefinitely

◎ **OPTIMAL STORAGE:** Airtight container in the refrigerator or freezer.

✳ **FREEZING:** Pure maple syrup, properly made, should not actually freeze, making the freezer a great place to store it as it will keep indefinitely. Store in an airtight container. Mix in any condensation on the top before use, and place back in the freezer after thawing, if desired.

↻ **USE IT UP/REVIVAL:** Maple syrup is graded according to color, sugar content, and flavor. Grade A is lighter and more delicately flavored and is typically poured directly onto foods, while Grades B and C are stronger in flavor and are used more for cooking and baking.

Maple syrup adds a nice richness to everything from Asian stir-fries to salad dressing. Try it in place of other sweeteners.

MAYONNAISE

▦ **REFRIGERATOR:** After opening

◉ **AT FRESHEST:** Commercial, unopened, 2 years; opened, 2 to 3 months

◎ **OPTIMAL STORAGE:** Commercial mayonnaise uses pasteurized eggs and has a high acidity level, which means it's in fact safe when stored at room temperature. However, quality and flavor are improved by keeping the jar in the refrigerator once opened.

✳ **FREEZING:** Not recommended.

↻ **USE IT UP/REVIVAL:** If the oil in mayonnaise has crystallized, stir gently and add a few drops of water, if necessary, to re-emulsify it.

NUT BUTTERS
(peanut butter, almond butter)

REFRIGERATOR: Yes

AT FRESHEST: Commercial, opened, 6 months; natural, opened, 3 months; unopened, 2 years

OPTIMAL STORAGE: Commercial nut butters can be kept in a cool, dry spot in the pantry but will last twice as long if kept in the refrigerator. Natural nut butters, once opened, should be stirred and then stored in the refrigerator in a sealed container.

FREEZING: Not recommended.

USE IT UP/REVIVAL: Over time, the oils in natural nut butters may separate into a layer at the top of the container. This is a natural process that does not affect the quality. Simply stir the oil back into the butter. Do not drain it off, as it will cause the butter to be overly dry.

Commercial peanut butter may be edible for much longer than listed here, but the quality will degrade.

Nut butters that have spoiled will smell "off" and should not be consumed.

OILS (olive, sesame, vegetable, coconut)

REFRIGERATOR: Sesame, yes; others, no

AT FRESHEST: Coconut oil—2 years in a cool, dark, dry place

Vegetable oil—Unopened, 1 year; opened, 2 months

Olive oil—Unopened, 2 years from harvest date; opened, 3 months

Sesame/flavorful nut oils—Unopened, 1 year; opened, 2 months

OPTIMAL STORAGE: All oils should be stored in a cool, dark, dry place.

For best quality, buy olive and vegetable oils in small quantities that you'll use within a couple of weeks. If you do buy larger amounts, transfer what you need for a week or two in the kitchen into a small, opaque bottle, and store the rest in a cool, dark place to minimize exposure to heat and light, then refill your small bottle as needed.

Coconut oil is a solid at room temperature and generally lasts longer than other oils.

Sesame oil and other flavorful nut oils are very sensitive and should be bought in small quantities and kept in the refrigerator after opening (but brought to room temperature before using).

FREEZING: Not beneficial/not recommended, though some products such as fresh herbs can be frozen in oil.

USE IT UP/REVIVAL: If oil begins to get rancid, it can still be put to good use. You can use it to polish and condition both wood furniture and leather shoes (wipe down the surface with a sponge to remove dust and grime, allow to dry, and then apply a light coat of olive oil, rubbing to allow the oil to fully soak in); to fix squeaky doors (use a rag to apply oil to the top of a problematic hinge); or to free stuck zippers (dab some olive oil on the zipper teeth).

Olive oil and coconut oil can be used to make homemade salt or sugar body scrubs.

Tidbit—We often think of olive oil as being shelf stable, but it's actually a perishable product. As a general rule, olive oil is best used within 1 to 2 years of pressing. Look for olive oils that are packaged in dark bottles and that list a harvest date. If no harvest date is listed, check the front and back labels to see where your oil is from. It the oil comes from far away, there is a greater chance that it will already have started to go rancid by the time it gets to you.

SPICES, DRIED AND GROUND

REFRIGERATOR: No

AT FRESHEST: Whole, up to 2 years; ground, up to 1 year

OPTIMAL STORAGE: Buy spices whole when you can and grind just before using. Also, buy them in small amounts. Keep in a cool, dark, dry place (not near the stove!) in airtight containers.

FREEZING: Not recommended.

USE IT UP/REVIVAL: Spices don't usually spoil, but they do lose potency over time. To test whether a ground spice is potent enough to be effective, rub a little between your fingers and taste/smell to see if the flavor and aroma are to your liking.

TEA

REFRIGERATOR: No

AT FRESHEST: Loose leaf, 6 to 9 months; tea bags: 2 years

OPTIMAL STORAGE: Loose leaf—Store in an airtight ceramic container or tin away from coffee and strong-smelling spices.

Tea bags—Store in original packaging in a cool, dry, dark place.

FREEZING: Not recommended.

USE IT UP/REVIVAL: Tea won't spoil, but it will lose potency and flavor over time.

Certain teas can be used to dye fabrics.

Bake cookies or quick breads and flavor them with dry tea.

Foodborne Illness

The more you can understand about what causes food to make you sick, the better armed you are to make decisions about how to care for your food and when it can be eaten with relatively low risk. Most foodborne illnesses are either infections from living microorganisms or toxins produced by these organisms or poisoning caused by harmful toxins. This section provides a bit more detail on these two main causes of foodborne illness.

Pathogens

While there are more than 250 types of foodborne illnesses, most are caused by *pathogens*, or microorganisms that cause disease. These include certain types of bacteria, viruses, parasites, and fungi. They also can include toxins created by these organisms. That's an important distinction to make, because while heating food to high temperatures can kill the organisms, some of the toxins they produce are chemicals that don't "die" and can therefore still be dangerous. Some also produce spores that can survive high heat and grow into cells when things cool down.

Ensuring that these organisms don't multiply into populations large enough to cause harm is a key step in keeping your food safe. Typically, a single bacterium won't make you sick. Most bacterial microbes need to multiply to a larger number before enough are present in food to cause disease.[61] (However, *Salmonella* can affect people even if the bacteria are present in only small populations.) Only certain conditions allow them to do this—and when those conditions are present, a single bacterium can produce 8 million progeny in 12 hours (if it reproduces by dividing itself every half hour). As a result, lightly contaminated food that wouldn't make you sick, if left out overnight, can be highly infectious by the next day. If the same food were refrigerated promptly, the bacteria would not multiply at all.

So as described in the "Smarter Storage" chapter, the name of the game is not giving microorganisms their desired conditions. In order to grow, pathogens need moisture, some kind of food or nutrients, the right temperature, enough time to grow, a low-acidity environment, and, for most, oxygen. High salt, high sugar, or high acid levels keep bacteria from growing, which is why salted meats, jam, and pickled vegetables are traditional preserved foods.

You don't need to remember all of that, though. In general, the way these pathogens lead to foodborne illness can be boiled down to three causes.

Time temperature abuse. Many foodborne illnesses happen because food has been "time temperature abused," meaning it was left for too long at temperatures that are good for the growth of pathogens. The "danger zone" is considered to be 41° to 135°F/5° to 57°C, but bacterial pathogens grow fastest at 70° to 125°F/21° to 52°C. Note that room temperature is about 72°F/22°C, which means that when you leave something on your countertop, you are leaving it at an ideal temperature for pathogen growth.

The longer food stays in the danger zone, the more time pathogens have to grow. This can happen when food is:

- Not stored at the right temperature (left out on the counter, left in a hot car, stored in a refrigerator that is above 40°F/4°C)

- Not cooked or reheated enough (think a quick microwave zap or leftovers brought on a picnic)

- Not cooled in the right way (a hot pot of soup gets left out overnight)

In general, refrigeration slows and freezing stops bacterial growth but does not kill anything. This means that as soon as they are returned to higher temperatures, they will become active

→» # Listeria

Listeriosis is a serious infection usually caused by eating food contaminated with the bacterium *Listeria monocytogenes*. This pathogen is an exception in that it can grow at refrigerated temperatures (below 40°F/4°C), whereas most pathogens cannot. Like other bacteria, it is killed on foods cooked at high temperatures. Therefore, it's mainly a problem associated with ready-to-eat foods. The sickness primarily affects older adults, pregnant women, newborns, and adults with weakened immune systems. However, rarely, persons

without these risk factors can also be affected. You can reduce the risk of listeriosis by following recommendations for safe food preparation, consumption, and storage. If you are in a high-risk group, you may also want to avoid certain high-risk foods such as deli meat. According to the FDA, foods with the highest risk of *Listeria* are:

- Deli meats
- Unheated hot dogs
- Paté and meat spreads
- Unpasteurized milk
- Smoked seafood
- Cooked, ready-to-eat crustaceans

again. One important exception to this rule is the bacterium *Listeria monocytogenes*, which can grow at refrigerated temperatures (see the "*Listeria*" box, page 189).

Cross-contamination. Pathogens can be transferred from one surface to another. While you'll be fine if you cook *Salmonella*-contaminated chicken to a high enough temperature, you're not going to cook the countertop you cut it on. Cross-contamination can occur whenever something contaminated touches something that is going to be eaten without being cooked first—think salads and already-cooked foods. In the kitchen, you can transfer microbes from one food to another food by using the same knife, cutting board, or other utensil to prepare both, without washing the surface or utensil in between. In addition, a food that is fully cooked can become recontaminated if it touches other raw foods or drippings from raw foods that contain pathogens.

Poor personal hygiene. Because some viruses are actually transferred by humans touching, coughing on, or sneezing on foods, a lack of hygiene in the kitchen can also lead to illness.

Toxins

There are essentially three types of toxins that could find their way into your food. The first is mentioned in the previous section: Toxins produced by microbes that remain toxic even after the microbes die. The second are those foods that naturally contain substances that are poisonous to humans, such as poisonous mushrooms or certain fish and shellfish. These are known as biotoxins. The last are synthetic chemicals that should not be in food in the first place but somehow get there, such as from a household cleaning product.

Pathogen-produced toxins. Bacteria and mold can produce toxins. These can remain even if the pathogens are killed. These types of toxins vary in their sensitivity to heat. Fortunately, the potent toxin that causes botulism is completely deactivated by boiling (hence the importance of boiling water baths when canning food at home). However, a different toxin produced by *Staphylococcus* bacteria (often shortened to "staph") is not deactivated even if it is boiled. The way to avoid illness from these toxins is to prevent the organisms from multiplying in the first place, which

→➤ Pasteurization

Named after its discoverer, Louis Pasteur, pasteurization is a heat treatment that extends the shelf life of milk and other foods by killing pathogenic and spoilage microbes and inactivating enzymes. There are different types of pasteurization that heat products up to varying temperatures for different lengths of time. Milk that is shelf stable has gone through "ultrahigh-temperature" pasteurization, thus allowing it to be stored for months without refrigeration. Most milk, fruit juices, and cheeses today are pasteurized. Eggs can be pasteurized at a low enough temperature to allow them to still be liquid, but most are not pasteurized.

means following the same steps you would follow to prevent pathogens. In addition, as mentioned in the "Can I Eat It?" chapter, moldy products should not be eaten unless you're able to remove ½ to 1 in/12 mm to 2.5 cm beyond the mold.

Biological toxins. Only certain foods are known to carry biological toxins:

FISH AND SHELLFISH can be toxic—for instance, certain parts of puffer fish. Clams, oysters, mussels, and scallops run the risk of carrying toxins. The most important step in avoiding these toxins is to purchase these foods from reputable sources.

A VARIETY OF WILD MUSHROOMS (not the types you see in the store) contain mushroom toxins. If you're buying wild mushrooms, be sure they're from a reputable source, and do not eat wild mushrooms unless a proven ninja mushroom expert stands in front of you and eats them first.

WILD PLANTS can have toxins too, so don't just eat anything you see while walking in the forest. What's crazy is that honey from bees that harvested pollen from toxic plants can also carry those toxins though this is quite rare. Again, just be careful where you buy your honey.

UNDERCOOKED KIDNEY BEANS, strangely enough, can carry a particular toxic substance that dissipates when they are fully cooked. White beans can carry this to a lesser extent. The bottom line is, be sure to cook your beans thoroughly.

Notes

1. K. D. Hall, J. Guo, M. Dore, and C. C. Chow, National Institute of Diabetes and Digestive and Kidney Diseases, "The Progressive Increase of Food Waste in America and Its Environmental Impact," *PLoS ONE* 4 no. 11 (2009), e7940.

2. J. Buzby et al., "The Estimated Amount, Value, and Calories of Postharvest Food Losses at the Retail and Consumer Levels in the United States," USDA Economic Research Service, *Economic Information Bulletin* 121, 2014.

3. K. D. Hall et al., "The Progressive Increase of Food Waste in America."

4. United Nations Food and Agricultural Organization, "Global Food Losses and Food Waste" (2011): www.fao.org/ag/ags/ags-division/publications/publication/en/?dyna_fef%5Buid%5D=74045.

5. L. Young, *The Portion Teller* (New York: Morgan Road Books, 2005), 9.

6. Large French fries were 167 grams in the United States and 150 grams in the United Kingdom according to McDonald's American and British websites at time of print.

7. L. Young and M. Nestle, "Expanding Portion Sizes in the U.S. Marketplace: Implications for U.S. Counseling." *Journal of the American Dietetic Association* 103, no. 2 (February 2003): portionteller.com/pdf/portsize.pdf.

8. National Heart, Lung, and Blood Institute, "Portion Distortion 2": www.nhlbi.nih.gov/health/public/heart/obesity/wecan/eat-right/portion-distortion.htm.

9. B. Wansink and K. van Ittersum, "Portion Size Me: Downsizing Our Consumption Norms," *Journal of the American Dietetic Association* 107, no. 7 (July 2007): 1103–1106.

10. B. Wansink and C. R. Payne, "The Joy of Cooking Too Much: 70 Years of Calorie Increases in Classic Recipes," *Annals of Internal Medicine*, 150 (2009): 291–292.

11. USDA, "Food Away from Home": www.ers.usda.gov/topics/food-choices-health/food-consumption-demand/food-away-from-home.aspx#.UosoJPldWeE.

12. D. Pimentel and M. Pimentel, "Sustainability of Meat-Based and Plant-Based Diets and the Environment," *American Journal of Clinical Nutrition* 78, no. 3 (September 2003): 660S–663S.

13. USDA Economic Research Service, "Major Uses of Land in the United States, 2007." Pub. 2011/EIB-89 (2011) www.ers.usda.gov/publications/eib-economic-information-bulletin/eib89.aspx#.UosgtPldWeE. Reports that 45 percent of the land is used for grazing and crop production combined.

14. M. A. Maupin et al., "Estimated use of water in the United States in 2010," U.S. Geological Survey Circular 1405, 2014.

15. The Water Footprint Network estimates that it takes 15,400 liters to produce 1 kilogram of beef (1,849 gallons per 1 pound). Assuming shower flow of 5 gl/19 L per 1 minute, this amounts to a 92-minute shower for a ¼ lb/ 115 g of beef. This estimate can vary quite a bit, depending on location and production methods.

16. M. Heller and G. Keoleian, "Greenhouse Gas Emission Estimates of U.S. Dietary Choices and Food Loss," *Journal of Industrial Ecology,* 2014. doi: 10.11-jiec. 12174.

17. U.S. EPA, "Municipal Solid Waste Generation, Recycling, and Disposal in the United States: Tables and Figures for 2012" for tonnage. Assumes $47/ton average tipping fees across country.

18. United Nations Food and Agriculture Organization, "Food Wastage Footprint: Impacts on Natural Resources," 2013.

19. *Ibid.*

20. *Ibid.*

21. United Nations World Food Programme, Hunger Statistics: www.wfp.org/hunger/stats.

22. C. Nellemann, M. MacDevett, T. Manders, B. Eickhout, B. Svihus, A. Prins, A. G., and B. P. Kaltenborn (eds), "The Environmental Food Crisis: The Environment's Role in Averting Future Food Crises. A UNEP Rapid Response Assessment." United Nations Environment Programme, February 2009: www.unep.org/pdf/foodcrisis_lores.pdf.

23. N. Alexandratos and J. Bruinsma, "World Agriculture Towards 2030/2050: The 2012 Revision," United Nations Food and Agricultural Organization, ESA Working Paper 12-03: www.fao.org/docrep/016/ap106e/ap106e.pdf.

24. Ibid.

25. B. Lipinski et al., "Reducing Food Loss and Waste," World Resources Institute, June 2013: www.wri.org/publication/creating-sustainable-food-future-installment-two.

26. R. Dobbs et al., "Resource Revolution: Meeting the World's Energy, Materials, Food, and Water Needs," McKinsey Global Institute, November 2011.

27. "Parliament Calls for Urgent Measures to Ban Food Waste in the E.U.," European Parliament News, January 19, 2012: www.europarl.europa.E.U./news/en/pressroom/content/20120118IPR35648/html/Parliament-calls-for-urgent-measures-to-halve-food-wastage-in-the-E.U.

28. This calculation assumes 2,600 calories per person per day and annual losses totaling 141 trillion calories, as reported in J. Buzby et al., "The Estimated Amount, Value, and Calories of Postharvest Food Losses."

29. Point of Purchase Advertising International, "2012 Shopper Engagement Study: Media Topline Report": www.popai.fr/textes/Shopper_Engagement_Study.pdf.

30. Ibid.

31. Point of Purchase Advertising International, "2012 Shopper Engagement Study": www.popai.fr/textes/Shopper_Engagement_Study.pdf.

32. Business Insider, "15 Ways Supermarkets Trick You Into Spending More Money": www.businessinsider.com/supermarkets-make-you-spend-money-2011-7?op=1#ixzz2uAiYAGEy.

33. WRAP UK, "Household Food and Drink Waste in the United Kingdom 2012": November 2013: www.wrap.org.uk/sites/files/wrap/hhfdw-2012-main.pdf.

34. The Kitchn, "15 Money-Saving Ways to Outsmart Your Supermarket": www.thekitchncom/15-moneysaving-ways-to-outsmart-your-supermarket-199531.

35. J. C. Rickman et al., "Nutritional Comparison of Fresh, Frozen and Canned Fruits and Vegetables. Part 1. Vitamins C and B and Phenolic Compounds," Journal of The Science of Food and Agriculture 87, no. 6 (April 2007): 930–944.

36. J. C. Rickman et al., "Nutritional Comparison of Fresh, Frozen, and Canned Fruits and Vegetables II. Vitamin A and Carotenoids, Vitamin E, minerals and fiber," Journal of The Science of Food and Agriculture 87, no. 7 (May 2007): 1185–1196.

37. Nutrition Action, "Should People Avoid Frozen Fish?": www.nutritionaction.com/daily/food-safety/should-people-avoid-frozen-fish.

38. National Geographic, "Frozen Seafood: In Many Ways, It's Better Than Fresh": ocean.nationalgeographic.com/ocean/take-action/frozen-seafood-benefits.

39. USDA, Food Safety and Inspection Service, "Freezing and Food Safety": www.fsis.usda/wps/portal/fsis/topics/food-safety-education/get-answers/food-safety-fact-sheets/safe-food-handling.

40. USDA, Food Safety and Inspection Service, "The Big Thaw—Safe Defrosting Methods for Consumers": www.fsis.usda.gov/wps/portal/fsis/topics/food-safety-education/get-answers/food-safety-fact-sheets/safe-food-handling/the-big-thaw-safe-defrosting-methods-for-consumers/CT_Index.

41. PR Newswire, "Home Canning Is Top Food Trend for Consumers Motivated to Eat Healthy, Fresh & Local": www.prnewswire.com/news-releases/home-canning-is-top-food-trend-for-consumers-motivated-to-eat-healthy-fresh--local-121995353.html.

42. National Center for Home Food Preservation, "Preserving Food at Home: A Self-Study": nchfp.uga.edu.

43. Much of the information in this section was gleaned from T. Zeryck et al., *How to Repair Food*, 3rd edition (Berkeley, CA: Ten Speed Press, 2010). It offers food-by-food instructions on fixing food disasters. I highly recommend it!

44. Centers for Disease Control and Prevention, "Food Safety: Prevention and Education": www.cdc.gov/foodsafety/prevention.html.

45. *Ibid.*

46. USDA, "Consumer-Level Food Loss Estimates and Their Use in the ERS Loss-Adjusted Food Availability Data," Pub. TB-927, 2011: www.ers.usda.gov/publications/tb-technical-bulletin/tb1927.aspx#.UotgFPldWeF.

47. Here's the math: Producing 1 pound of turkey meat releases 5 kilograms of carbon dioxide equivalent emissions, according to the Environmental Working Group, and uses 520 gallons of water (if it's similar to chicken production as estimated by the Water Footprint Network). At 423 grams of carbon dioxide equivalent per mile, as estimated by the United States EPA, that's a per-pound equivalent of driving your car 11 miles and taking a 130-minute shower (at 4 gallons per minute). U.S. consumers purchased around 736 million pounds of turkey in 2013, according to the National Turkey Federation, of which about 581 million pounds will be actual meat, assuming 21 percent of each turkey is inedible, as estimated by the USDA. Using the USDA estimate of 35 percent consumer loss for turkey, that amounts to 204 million pounds of meat discarded. Multiplied by the amounts per pound given earlier, that equates to a total of about 1 million tons of carbon dioxide equivalent and 105 billion gallons of water with it. New York City consumes about 1 billion gallons of water per day, according to the city's water consumption data, and San Francisco is 2,915 miles from New York, according to Google. The USDA defines a serving as 3 to 4 ounces of lean meat—4 ounces were used for this calculation. 17.6 million households in the United States are food insecure according to the USDA.

Sources:

· Environmental Working Group, "Meat Eater's Guide to Climate Change and Health; Methodology" (2011): static.ewg.org/reports/2011/meateaters/pdf/methodology_ewg_meat_eaters_guide_to_health_and_climate_2011.pdf.

· Water Footprint Network, Product Gallery Water Footprint Estimates: www.waterfootprint.org/?page=files/productgallery&product=chicken.

· National Turkey Federation, "Turkey Facts and Trivia": www.eatturkey.com/why-turkey/history.

· USDA, "Consumer-Level Food Loss Estimates."

· NYC Open Data, "Water Consumption in New York City": data.cityofnewyork.us/Environment/Water-Consumption-In-The-New-York-City/ia2d-e54m.

· USDA, "Household Food Security in the United States in 2012": www.ers.usda.gov/media/1183204/err-155-report-summary.pdf.

48. USDA, Food Safety and Inspection Service, "The Color of Meat and Poultry": www.fsis.usda.gov/wps/portal/fsis/topics/food-safety-education/get-answers/food-safety-fact-sheets/meat-preparation/the-color-of-meat-and-poultry/the-color-of-meat-and-poultry/CT_Index.

49. University of Illinois Extension, "Bacterial Soft Rot of Vegetables, Fruits, and Ornamentals," *Reports on Plant Diseases*, no. 943 (1990).

50. H. McGee, *On Food and Cooking: The Science and Lore of the Kitchen* (New York, Simon and Schuster, 2007).

51. E. B. Leib and D. Gunders, "The Dating Game: How Confusing Date Labels Lead to Food Waste in America," Harvard Law School and Natural Resources Defense Council, 2013.

52. Foodsafety.gov, "Who's at Risk": www.foodsafety.gov/poisoning/risk.

53. ASPCA, "Feeding Your Adult Dog": www.aspca.org/pet-care/dog-care/feeding-your-adult-dog.

54. M. Nestle and M. C. Nesheim, *Feed Your Pet Right: The Authoritative Guide to Feeding Your Dog and Cat* (New York: Free Press, 2010), 244.

55. *Ibid.*, 251.

56. CNN Eatocracy, "F.A.Q. About the Backyard Chicken Boom," eatocracy.cnn.com/2012/04/11/f-a-q-about-the-backyard-chicken-boom/comment-page-2.

57. Michigan State University Extension, "Homemade Cleaners": www.msue.msu.edu/objects/content_revision/download.cfm/revision_id.499694/workspace_id.-4/01500631.html.

58. T. DiStefano and L. Belenky, "Life-Cycle Analysis of Energy and Greenhouse Gas Emissions from Anaerobic Biodegradation of Municipal Solid Waste," *Journal of Environmental Engineering* 135, no. 11 (November 2009), 1097–1105.

59. Washington Post, "Curbside Composting": www.washingtonpost.com/national/health-science/curbsidecomposting/2013/02/03/8d4481f2-6e62-11e2-ac36-3d8d9dcaa2e2_graphic.html.

60. Information for this Directory came from a large variety of sources. I leaned heavily on the following.

· Food safety information from the FDA and USDA Food Safety and Inspection Service. Some of this can be found on www.foodsafety.gov and at www.fsis.usda.gov/wps/portal/fsis/topics/food-safety-education/get-answers/food-safety-fact-sheets.

· The University of Georgia's National Center for Home Food Preservation: nchfp.uga.edu.

· Cooperative Extension information, such as that of Utah State University: extension.usu.edu/foodstorage and Virginia Polytechnic Institute and State University: pubs.ext.vt.edu/348/348-960/348-960_pdf.pdf.

· H. McGee, *On Food and Cooking: The Science and Lore of the Kitchen* (New York: Scribner, 2004).

· C. Williams, *Williams-Sonoma Kitchen Companion: The A to Z Guide to Everyday Cooking Equipment & Ingredients* (Des Moines, IA: Oxmoor House, 2002).

· Information from producers of products and trade associations.

61. Centers for Disease Control and Prevention, "Food Safety": www.cdc.gov/foodsafety/facts.html.

Index